THE LEARNING JOURNEY

STORYTELLING AS A DESIGN PRINCIPLE
TO CREATE POWERFUL LEARNING EXPERIENCES

Bastian Küntzel

The Learner's Journey

Storytelling as a Design Principle to create powerful Learning Experiences.

Author BASTIAN KÜNTZEL
Copyediting CHRISTIAN DUMAIS
Cover Design and Illustrations MICHAL WRONSKI
Layout ANNA POMICHOWSKA

I received extensive feedback from Dorota Mołodyńska-Küntzel, Alex Jbeily and Alex Neumann for which I am profoundly thankful.
Andreas Karsten, Anna-Maria Hass, Anna Pomichowska, Viola Thuma, Elisa Gazzotti, Birgit Mohai, Sneszana Baccijl-Koch, and Marcos Tourinho also read early drafts and I'm thankful for their comments and encouragement.

Bibliografische Information der Deutschen Nationalbibliothek:
Die Deutsche Nationalbibliothek verzeichnet diese Publikation in der Deutschen Nationalbibliografie, detaillierte bibliografische Daten sind in Internet über http://dnd.dnb.de abrufbar.

I wrote this for you.
I hope you like it.

Hello World,

I love *Sendung mit der Maus,* a children's TV programme in Germany that explains how things are made and work. I watched it as a child and now my children watch it with me. I've probably watched the making of *The Lord of the Rings* more often than I watched the actual movie. I just love to know how the things I cherish get made.

I recently stumbled across a theory that explained how something that I have been enjoying for a long time worked: stories. My whole life I've loved movies from Terrence Hill and Bud Spencer Italo Westerns to *The Godfather* to Peter Jackson's *The Lord of the Rings* adaptations. When I watch a film, you cannot talk to me. I'm not there - I'm in the movie. The same is true for me with novels. As each *Harry Potter* book came out, I read it instantaneously, completely sucked into the experience.

I am, of course, far from alone as a story enthusiast. Everyone seemingly loves stories, otherwise there'd be no publishing industry, no Hollywood, no Bollywood, no TED and no bedtime reading rituals with our kids.

A tech leader I follow on Twitter, Michael Loop (@rands) recently put it very nicely: "Story is the fundamental human currency." People worldwide tell stories, listen to stories, and make sense of their lives and communicate powerful insights through stories. Stories resonate so much because we experience our lives as stories and ourselves as the protagonist in their centre. We identify with the protagonists of the stories we consume either because they are similar to us and the experiences we've had, or because they reflect who and how we would like to be.

The theory I bumped into was the *monomyth* or the *hero's journey* – two expressions for the same concept originally developed by Joseph Campbell. I also came across the work of screenwriter/director Dan Harmon, who had studied Campbell's work and had developed his own simplified approach to story structure based on it: the story circle.

My first reaction to learning about Harmon's theory was "Wow, this is so cool!" I can't watch movies anymore without constantly thinking about the meta-level of where we are in the story circle and how each protagonist's journey is presented. And it doesn't ruin the experience for me - it improves it. I love it!

After the initial shock of "Wow, this is so cool!" passed, I realised that most, if not all, great learning experiences that I've had followed the same steps as were laid out in this theory.

Since then I've used Harmon's version of the story circle as a framework for developing very different educational experiences for very different groups. I've designed management retreats for eight people, conferences for over a hundred people, training courses for 20 people, and strategic planning workshops for 40 people – all using this framework.

And it always worked fantastically.

I call this approach *The Learner's Journey*.

A short note on terminology use, my approach to popular stories and who this book is for

I'm going to be using the term *learning event* as an umbrella for any type of organised learning - whether that be a conference, seminar, lesson, workshop, retreat or training.

I'm going to use *learning facilitator* to refer to anyone that is charged with planning, leading and influencing this process - teachers, trainers, facilitators, moderators, coaches, professors or lecturers. And the term participant for anyone who is consciously attending to learn something, such as pupils, students, attendees or, well, training course participants.

I use popular stories to make my point about the universality of the structure of stories and how they relate to the process of designing learning events. Popular as in - I love them. So if you don't like *Star Wars*, *Harry Potter*, *Moana* (known to my family and many others as *Vaiana*), *The Blues Brothers*, *The Lord of the Rings* or *Notting Hill*. Humour me.

The basic structure works with your favourite stories as well, so if you get annoyed with my favourites, I invite you to use your own examples.

I wrote this book as a contribution to my community of praxis. I hope that it will be a valuable and meaningful contribution to the development of environments, experiences and situations where learning can take place in safe but challenging ways.

If the framework I am offering here can help learning facilitators to remove some of the barriers for learning - it would make me very happy indeed.

15

PART I
Story - the basic
human currency

16

The Power of Story

22

The Actual
Hero's Journey

26

The Story Circle
as a Journey
of Transformation

33

PART II
Setting the scene

34

Situating learning

39

Stakeholder

45

Needs

50

Context

69

PART III
The learning flow –
building the story

70

PHASE I:
Purposeful
Departure

74

PHASE II:
Exploration

76

PHASE III:
Transformative
Integration

78

PROTAGONIST
"I see you"

86

NEED
"The Gap"

92

GO
"The Jump"

96

SEARCH
"The Challenge"

104

FIND
"The Encounter"

108

TAKE
"The Incorporation"

113

RETURN
"The Integration"

117

CHANGE
"The new normal"

121

PART IV
Some
concrete examples

125

The 2nd
International
Youth Volunteering
Conference
of UNESCO

129

Authentic Authority
Management Retreat
for a global
financial institution

135

Mission, Vision
and Values Workshop
for an international
aviation company

1

Story - the basic human currency

The Power of Story   p. 16

The actual Hero's Journey   p. 22

The Story Circle as a Journey of
Transformation   p. 26

PART I: Story - the basic human currency

The Power of Story

As soon as humans started to communicate, they told stories. You can go visit cave-paintings that are thousands and thousands of years old and you'll see stories that are being told visually. Some of the earliest human writings also tell stories. We don't know what people talked about once talking became a thing, but chances are there were many stories being told around the fire in the evenings.

That's because, as humans, we experience the world around us not as impulses of light and sound that we take in through our senses, but rather as something more than that: we experience it as a reality that has a meaning we can make sense of. The world around us makes no sense by itself. We make sense of it by embedding what we experience into a story.

Identity is the story we tell ourselves about ourselves. It has been well established that, particularly in conflicts, we might resort to tell a victim story about ourselves, or a helplessness story, i.e. that we have no other choice but to act with aggression, retreat or whatever else we need to justify doing something to someone else. We also explain other people's behaviour in terms of stories: "Ah yes, she behaves this way because she is terribly in love with her neighbour, but her aunt just died, who had harboured a life-long love for this person as well, and now she has a guilty conscience because..."[1]

In fact, deprive any situation of its history and context and it

---

[1] The excellent book Crucial Conversations by Kerry Patterson, Joseph Grenny, Ron McMillan and Al Switzler goes into a lot more depth in this, highlighting also how crucial it is to understand the story we subconsciously tell ourselves, and to have empathy for the stories others might tell themselves, in order to solve conflicts and speak about uncomfortable issues.

becomes downright weird. Most of what we do, say, or react to in any particular way is saturated with the continuous story that provides everything with meaning.

In Yuval Noah Harari's book *Sapiens*, he makes the point that the evolution of homo sapiens stopped being biological at some point and became cultural.

Humans didn't need to adjust physically to the changing environments they lived in to the degree other species did. Their adaptability was catalysed and amplified from what they could learn from their ancestors and they in turn from their ancestors through the stories they passed on.

Instead of needing to change our digestive and sensory organs to the food that was available, and our instincts to the predators that were out to get us, we could simply talk and listen. People could learn from the stories that were told to them from their peers, the scouts that went out to search for new resources, and the elders who'd seen it all, and thus adapt rapidly. It was no longer necessary to observe and learn from everything directly. Language and our ability to tell and comprehend stories gave us an incredible evolutionary advantage and we came to dominate every environment we entered (for better or worse).

Every conversation tells a story, sometimes explicitly, sometimes implicitly. Every comment someone makes gets inserted into the story we tell ourselves about that person and every experience we make becomes a part of the *mythology of ourselves*.

I think of this self-mythology as a body of experiences, ideas and self-perceptions that give a sense to who we are today, what is good and bad, and what is the mental-model we use to see ourselves in the world. The experiences we think back on with pride are most often those we might turn into the major plot points of our own story. Mental breakdowns, personal crises and periods of confusion are often moments when we're not sure if the story we've been telling about ourselves is the one we want or should be telling.

Psychologist Daniel Kahneman distinguishes between the *'experiencing self* and the *'remembering self*. The *'experiencing self* is basically us in the now, taking in the environmental stimuli and immediately processing them. In his words:

"...the remembering self is a storyteller. And that really starts with a basic response of our memories -- it starts immediately. We don't only tell stories when we set out to tell stories. Our memory tells us stories, that is, what we get to keep from our experiences is a story."[2]

It is, of course, nothing revolutionary to claim that stories are important. But it is quite remarkable just how fundamental stories are to our lives. It's not only when we sit down for a good book, watch a movie or read a fairy tale to our children that stories surround us. It's all the time.

Observe children and you can see how a great part of their play is impersonating different characters: from being mum and dad to a cat to a super-hero.

On my children's birthday, they receive a photo-album of their previous year. So they each have a row of albums on a shelf essentially telling their story that grows a new volume every year. They love looking at them. When guests visit, the kids routinely take their albums out and show them their story.

We're constantly explaining our and other's behaviour in terms of story - the hero, the villain, the helper, the stupid-but-fun-sidekick, etc. That's because we have no choice but to

---

[2] He said this in his 2010 TED Talk "The riddle of experience vs. memory". I also heard him speak about this on *The TED Interview* podcast in the episode: "Daniel Kahneman wants you to doubt yourself".

think of ourselves and others in these terms. They are how we navigate this complex world around us and find our place in it.

And that makes a lot of sense, given what stories provide. When you read about soap or lavender, in addition to the cortex in your brain that interprets symbols such as letters, the olfactory cortex also lights up. So when we are reminded in the abstract about something we have physically experienced in the past (smelling lavender, for example), our brain resurfaces those experiences and makes it come to life. We can literally smell lavender when we read about lavender.

When you read about movements, the motor-cortex lights up. When you read about other people's emotions, the emotional centre of the brain, the limbic system, is active. Reading, watching or listening to stories give us a chance to experience someone else's life, literally experience it, without having to be in it.[3]

People who read a lot of fiction or watch movies have a better capacity for *theory of mind*, meaning the ability to know what others might be thinking or feeling at this moment. This empathy is a crucial skill in navigating our complex social environments.

All this is to say that stories naturally work on us as humans. Stories suck us in, catch our attention and keep us interested in what's happening next. And we're looking for the story of what's going on; unconsciously, most of the time, but relentlessly.

What does all of this talk about stories have to do with learning?

---

[3] The brain mechanics involved in this probably include so called *mirror neurons* – neurons that fire when you do something as well as when you observe someone else doing something. This means that by observing someone doing something, our brain is behaving as if we were doing that same thing. This is proven in monkeys, but not yet definitive in humans. It is, however, very likely that we work in very similar ways.

Well, my contention is that in powerful learning experiences, the learners actually see themselves as the protagonists of a story of transformation.

Think about it - what was your most powerful learning experience? What was the struggle you had to go through? What was the context you came from and how did those new competences you were developing going to be impacting that context? Did you have a guide or companion, someone you trusted, but who would also challenge you and push you farther than you thought you could go?

If I take the learning experiences that I've had and that are still with me today and I overlay the structure of stories, it's a real good fit. Learning experiences are stories. And as learning facilitators we can learn from the principles of good storytelling and apply them as design principles into our programme design. The learners participating in our learning events will be framing the experience in a story about themselves anyway, so we might as well structure what we're planning to do within their framework.

Storytelling has historically been used as an educational tool. The most explicit example are case-studies where the story of what happened to someone is literally right there on paper and used to analyse the decisions of the protagonist(s). Through this process, learners hope to gain a deeper understanding of the dynamics and influences that led to the outcome it did. You can't write the word history without story. Even in math or physics lessons, good teachers tell gripping stories of how, for example, two trains are running towards each other at different speeds and we could prevent a tragedy if we can determine where exactly they will collide.

The Learner's Journey is not about how to use storytelling as a method, such as a case-study, an anecdote during a presentation, or a simulation. Of course, knowing how good stories are constructed will help you tell better stories as you run your trainings, teach your seminars or give your talk.

But what if we think of these learning events AS a story that you and the learners are the protagonists of? And how about designing the learning path along the basic core structure that every story ever told has as its skeleton? I've done this a bunch of times now and I couldn't be happier with the results.

Let me tell you how.

The actual Hero's Journey

Decades ago, Joseph Campbell laid the foundations for truly understanding the universal nature of almost every story ever told in his 1949 work *The Hero with a Thousand Faces*. In it, he developed the concept of the *monomyth* or the *hero's journey*. He theorised that most great stories, regardless of when or where they were written or told, follow the same pattern. Each story, according to Campbell, is essentially about a hero going on a journey towards and through the unknown, who then emerges later having changed and bringing change back to their original environment.

Campbell was a very spiritual man, a trained theologian but far from dogmatic. He became fascinated with the stories and myths of Native Americans, as well as the core mythological stories of the Maori, among many others. He deeply dove into Hinduism, Buddhism, Judaism and Islam. He learned that some of the core themes were remarkably similar across religions, even if they have never had any interaction, exchange or mutual influence.

At the core of this are shared human experiences that span recorded history: how life leads to death and how from death new life emerges. How light (day) turns into darkness (night) which turns into light again. How trees and plants decay and turn into the stuff that new life is made from. With all this input, no wonder humans started to tell and respond to stories that follow that same logic of circular transformation.

Campbell divides the hero's journey into three phases, each one with a few sub-steps. These phases are *departure, initiation,* and *return.*

Within the departure phase, the steps are
- Call to Adventure
- Refusal of the Call
- Supernatural Aid
- Crossing the First Threshold
- Belly of the Whale

During initiation we have
- The Road of Trials
- The Meeting with the Goddess
- The Woman as Temptress
- Atonement with the Father
- Apotheosis
- The Ultimate Boon

Finally, in the return phase we have
- Refusal of the Return
- The Magic Flight
- Rescue from Without
- The Crossing of the Return Threshold
- Master of Two Worlds
- Freedom to Live

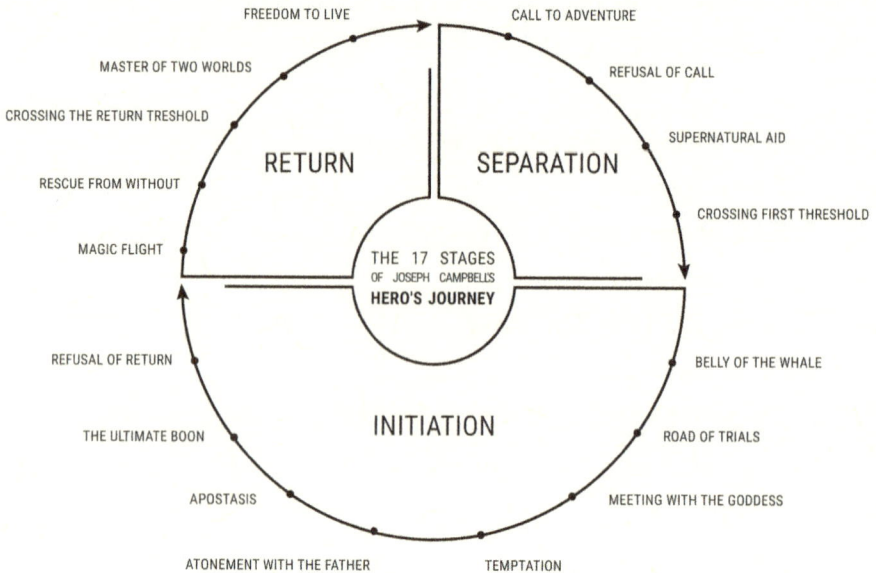

These steps, or their variations, can be found in almost all of the big stories, the myths of old and new that provide guidance and moral education - from *The Bible* to *The Odyssey* to Greek mythology and the fundamental tales of Hinduism. Some of the steps, of course, are quite specific, so it's important to remember that these are metaphors. Not every story explicitly has Supernatural Aid, The Woman as Temptress and Atonement with the Father. But many stories, from romantic comedies to action thrillers go through these steps with some predictability.

George Lucas, a good friend and student of Campbell's work used the Hero's Journey in this form very closely in his work. Going through the steps of Campbell's Hero's Journey is almost like reading the outline of the script for the original *Star Wars* trilogy. I know people who have used Campbell's framework as a basis for training courses, but for me it's too specific; too detailed. Also, obviously, the gendered tone of the stages is problematic as well.

Years later, Dan Harmon, a screenwriter and Campbell savant, broke down the concept of the Hero's Journey into a simplified structure that, he argues, every story goes through - even stupid ones.[4] Harmon isn't a scholar and maybe not quite as spiritual as Campbell was. His innovation, as far as I see it, is that he took the structure of the Hero's Journey out of the mythological realm and applied it to writing sitcoms, fart-jokes and comedies.

And because of its simplicity, it is more adaptable and understandable than Campbell's original theory. It's Harmon's story circle that, ultimately, I'm using as the basic underlying structure to plan and implement learning events.

If you're intrigued by Campbell, I implore you to get and read *The Hero with a Thousand Faces*. It's a great book. But I'm not going to spend any more time on it here, because, you know, focus.

---

[4] He laid this out in a series of short and highly entertaining texts online. Start with https://channel101.fandom.com/wiki/Story_Structure_101:_Super_Basic_Shit and go from there.

The Story Circle as a Journey of Transformation

Draw a circle - that's your story. Divide it in an upper half and a lower half. The upper half is the light, the known, order and life. The lower part is the dark, the unknown, chaos and death.

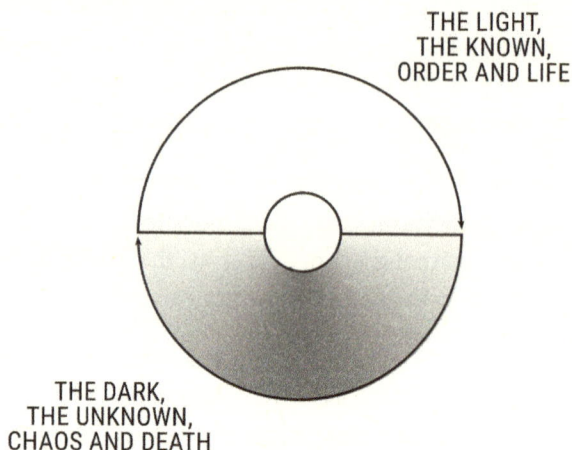

THE LIGHT,
THE KNOWN,
ORDER AND LIFE

THE DARK,
THE UNKNOWN,
CHAOS AND DEATH

Every story starts in the known, compels its protagonist to go into the unknown, where they struggle or explore and ultimately grow. They then need to bring this new version of themselves full of new insights and growth back into the light, into the known normality, so that the new and the old can be integrated into a changed and new reality.

This makes a lot of sense because this is how life is. We're born out of the matter of our parents, and when we die we become a part of the matter of the earth again, which transforms and slowly moves the molecules to create new life. It goes round and round from life to death and back again.

It's also how we progress in life. Few discoveries have been made in the known. We learn the most when we enter a space that is unknown and where we have a distinct need and incentive to turn this unknown into the known and internalise it so that we can bring it back into our own world.

Every myth, every religious story, every romantic comedy and every action-thriller follows this path.

Siddhartha leaves his palace, sees and does a lot of stuff, sits under a tree a lot, resists temptations, and comes back as the Buddha. Neo is given the chance to leave the known world and see the truth, learns how to kick ass, meets the Oracle and finally, after more ass-kicking, accepts his new self as the Chosen One. Luke and Rey leave their respective home planets, learn that they're special and start fighting the dark forces and finally return as their new selves in the realm of the Rebellion. Your aunt goes on a vacation, where she steps on a bee on the beach, it hurts a lot, but she meets a nice fellow traveller in the doctor's waiting room, they fall in love and now she is moving to Iowa.

Always the same: the protagonist leaves, gets pushed beyond their comfortable boundaries, learns something about themselves and returns changed.

Stop for a second here and see if this works on a story you love. I bet it does.

It's not that this great story recipe was gifted to someone at some point and then everyone went like: "Great - let's do it this way from now on!" No, every great story follows this structure because life follows this structure. Plants and flowers arrive in spring, flourish during summer and die in autumn to be resurrected again the following spring. Each one of us will experience that a loved one dies and is forever gone, but each one of us will also experience that new loved ones will enter our lives in the most unexpected ways. It's only logical that the stories which are told to make sense of this experience of the world follow the same structure as life does.

Let's turn our focus back to learning for a moment. Following the story circle doesn't mean that learning needs to be unpleasant, dark or dangerous. Far from it. The metaphor of *comfort*, *stretch* and *panic-zones*[5] is useful here. It states that when learners are in their comfort zone, they are not going to develop and learn anything new because they are too comfortable in their own perspective. If they are in their panic zone, they are also not going to be able to learn because their primal instincts and stress-response mechanisms in the brain are taking over to focus on survival. In that state it's not possible to think, reflect, or abstract. The stretch zone is the ideal zone for learning, but it needs to provide space and opportunities to return to the comfort zone as well as clear strategies to increase the comfort zone in order to occupy the space that was once stretching. Challenging enough to expand our horizons, to stretch us, but safe enough to allow us to actually think about what's happening.

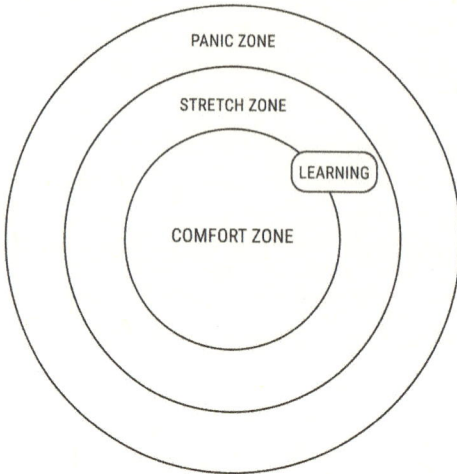

PANIC ZONE

STRETCH ZONE

LEARNING

COMFORT ZONE

Prof. Amy Edmondson's concept of psychological safety is handy here too. She argues that teams work best when members feel safe to make mistakes, challenge each other in the spirit of mutual support and hold each other to high standards because

---

[5] Outdoor and adventure educator Karl Rohnke is attributed with coming up with this concept.

they believe in each other's abilities to reach them.[6] I would say that learning follows the same logic. We need the challenge to push us, while feeling safe enough to be pushed to where we have never been before. Accompanied by someone who believes in our ability to make it there and back again.

After dividing the circle into the upper half and the lower half - now divide it into the right side and the left side. The right side is the journey there and the left side is the journey back. Seems obvious as far as journeys go.

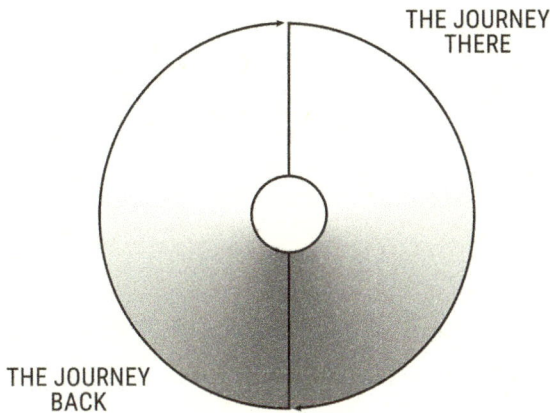

THE JOURNEY
THERE

THE JOURNEY
BACK

These four inflection points are really key moments of any experience of growth and development. The transition from the known into the unknown is hard, it's unpleasant and it requires motivation. But similarly, the decision to return, the change of direction from tumbling down to moving upwards back into the known can be hard. Whatever competence, skill or insight has been discovered in the chaos of learning, makes sense in that very context. To take it on, to grab it and say

---

[6] If you want to learn more about this, I would suggest you read her book *Teaming: How Organisations Learn, Innovate, and Compete in the Knowledge Economy.*

"You're part of me now!" and then invite it to become part of who the learners are in the known world – that takes resolve.

Finally, the transition back into the known can be quite the struggle. There will be opposition from their old reality to the insights and creations that we bring from the darkness. Of course - it doesn't belong there; it wasn't part of it before.

At each of these borders, the learners are dealing with real barriers that we need to address consciously and purposefully.

So these four points, these border, mark actually four stages of the story circle that Dan Harmon proposed. Overall, he reduced Campbell's 17 steps to just 8. They are: Protagonist, Need, Go, Search, Find, Take, Return, and Change. Much easier to remember, if you ask me. And these are the 8 steps that I'm using for The Learner's Journey.

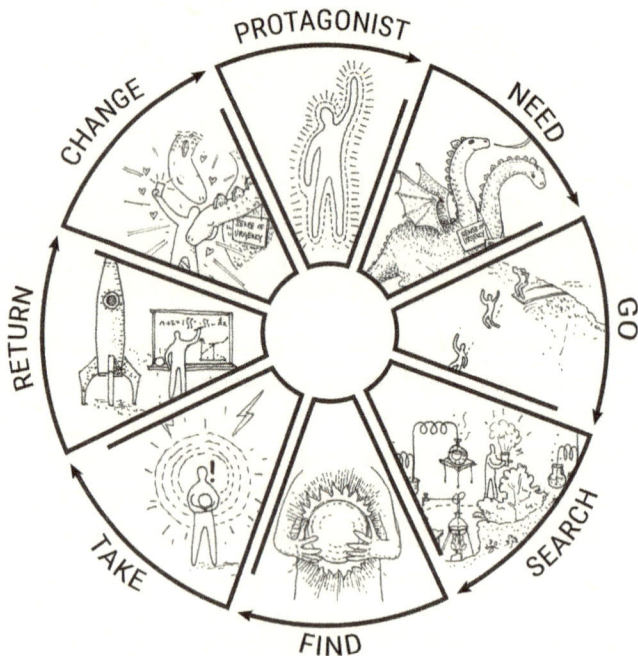

When learning facilitators use the story circle as a framework for developing learning events, it allows us to design an educational experience that follows the same path along which our learners themselves experience. Ideally, we're not working against the natural flow and momentum of our participants, but we're providing a logical journey where each step reasonably follows the previous one and is laying the foundation for what's next. By using the basic story structure as a design principle for creating learning events, we can develop a story of transformation alongside our participants where they are the heroes.

Using the Learner's Journey is not about fitting a learning programme into a set structure. Instead, it's about utilizing the structure of the human experience of transformation to facilitate learning.

2

Setting the Scene

Situating Learning   p. 34

Stakeholder   p. 39

Needs   p. 45

Context   p. 50

PART II: Setting the Scene
Situating Learning

Let's consider for a moment about what learning actually is.

To me, learning is transformation. At the mechanical, biological, neurological level, learning happens when the connections between different neurons are strengthened and the impulses from one to the other can go quicker and farther.

If we want to know something, or remember what we have once heard or read, we need to make those excitations between neurons persistent so that they are more easily available in the future when we need them. Neuroscientists call this long-term potentiation.

What we know from numerous studies is that moderate stress, the good and stimulatory stress, encourages long-term potentiation between neutrons at the synaptic level. Prolonged stress, the kind that makes you sick, depressed and gives you tics and pains, actually leads to what's called *long-term depression*, a weakening of connections that lowers how much and how well we can think and remember new facts.[7]

It's not a stretch to say then that learning literally physically transforms our brain. Neurons make new connections and strengthen the ones they have. In order to do that they need a stimulating environment that repeats this new information in different ways until it has become part of the transformed brain's architecture.

---

[7] I learned about this from the excellent book *Behave* by Robert Sapolsky. He specifically references the article "Long-Term Potentiation: Peeling the Onion" by R. Nicoll and K. Roche, which was published in Volume 74 of *Neuropharmacology* in 2013.

What this means is that we, as learning facilitators, need to find the right balance between challenge and safety, between the novel and the repetition of what we've said already, between the map of knowledge, skills and attitudes that already exist in the brain and the new ones we aim to add through our programmes.

To achieve this, it's important that we place the learning event firmly into the world of our participants so that it can become a part of their story that makes sense for them. We can't ask participants to see themselves as the protagonists of a story that has nothing to do with their reality. It provides the context and the purpose for learning and a connection point to the content of our learning journey.

And every learner has their own world. Every learner has passions and interests. Every learner has an image of themselves of who they are and who they would like to be. Every learner is embedded in a context that includes challenges, dreams, values and ambitions.

Someone who loves hip-hop is probably going to be more excited to play Bach in their piano lessons when they discover that plenty of amazing hip-hop producers use tons of classical music elements as samples or inspiration. A person with a highly analytical mind might need hard data and scientific evidence to highlight that the position in the company they strive to get might require them to invest some time in reflecting on their soft-skills. The founder of a company might feel very protective of the organisation they have built and their products but needs to let go of control if she wants it to grow. If we want to really maximise the learning potential of whatever format we're engaged in, then we ignore the world of the learners at our peril.

Rarely is a learning event a relation purely between participant and learning facilitator. Not even a deeply personal coaching process, in most cases, is a simple two-way relation between coach and client. Most learning events have several stakeholders. Those that participate in it. Those that pay for it. Those that organise it. Those that benefit from it secondarily i.e. when we train trainers, teachers, or youth workers, managers, or organisational leaders.

Each of these stakeholders has their specific world that influences what they expect from, what they're able to give to and what they need from the learning event.

If we want to create learning events that are impactful beyond the training/conference/class-room, we need to balance the needs of those different stakeholders and have a clear and realistic view on how much of this can be achieved in the time and space that is available. We need to make sure that the different stakeholders can see that their needs are met by making it about something that's explicitly and implicitly meaningful and responding to the world they operate in.

Throughout all this, we need to remain aware of the necessary conditions that allow for learning to happen and the story that we tell throughout the learning journey that pulls everyone in, gives them the forward momentum they need and is consistently worth the attention of the learners.

It's not easy. In fact, it's very difficult. But it's difficult in the way that all good and worthy things in life are difficult.

When I meet with a client to plan a learning event, I typically structure that conversation along four main points:

- Stakeholders (Who are they and what are their needs and expectations towards the event? What is their version of a world worth working towards - their destination?)

- Context (What are the limiting factors in terms of time, space and materials? What are the unique opportunities?)

- Content (What does the event need to be about, explicitly and implicitly, to address most of the stakeholders needs?)

- Story (What is the journey that the participants need to take in order to reach their destination successfully?)

STAKEHOLDERS

NEEDS

CONTEXT

THE LEARNER'S
JOURNEY

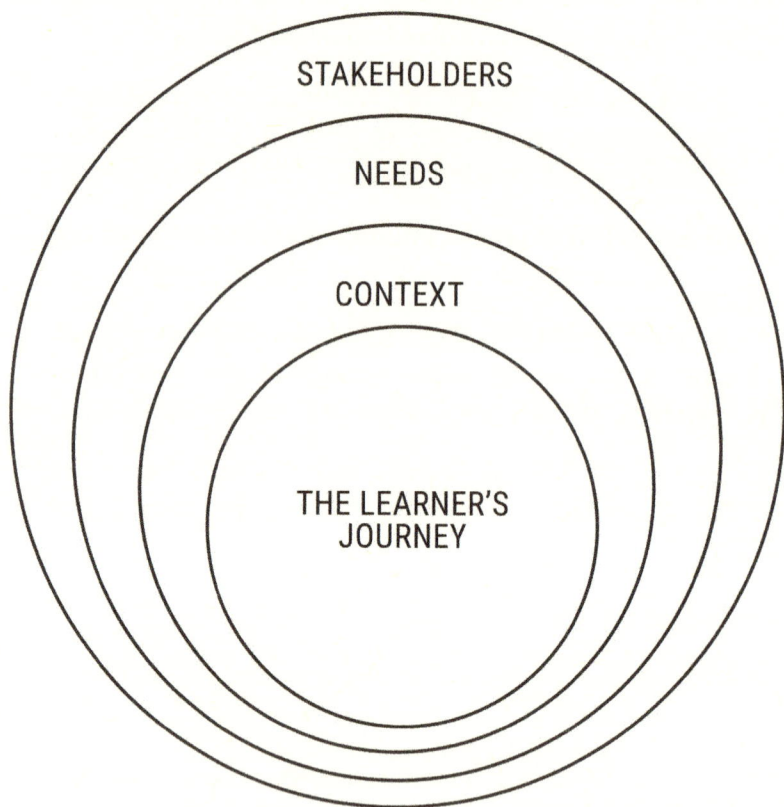

It isn't really possible to develop the Story part, the actual learning programme, without a deep awareness about the world the story is set in. So let's now look at the *Stakeholders*, their *Needs* (*regarding the content and the results*) and the *Context* and for a moment before diving deeper into the *Story* part.

Stakeholder

In most (dare I say all?) organised learning situations, the participants are not the only ones who have expectations regarding the outcomes of the events. There are more stakeholders at play that invest different resources - time, money, expertise, effort - and who have certain expectations towards the outcome in order to merit their investments.

It is very important to align and negotiate the needs of the stakeholders to have tangible outcomes. A skilled learning facilitator will not promise outcomes they can't stand behind or are impossible to achieve with the time and resources given.

The question we need to answer for ourselves is: what brings these different stakeholders together to make their time, money, effort or headspace available to support this learning event?

My answer is: it must be important, if not necessary, for them. There must be an actual need that we're addressing and a conscious (or unconscious) awareness that the world (or they, as part of that world) are going to be better after they've engaged in the learning process.

A large organisation might want to further the understanding of a specific phenomenon by bringing together a bunch of experts to discuss it and then present a report. A school band might want to have their songs on Spotify so that they can stream it at the school party. An athlete might want to be able to finish that race and be respected in her community of sports enthusiasts or just enjoy her post-workout high.

What this *better* is, is entirely subjective, by the way. A person spending hours playing the piano and a person practicing how to shoot a gun are going to be driven by the same thought: the future version of themselves who are better at their craft is a version worth investing time, effort and money into.

Looking around at the faces in any given fitness studio, we won't find a lot of smiles. Instead we'll see pressure, concentration and, yes, pain. Why are they doing this then? Because the body they could live in seems more desirable than the one they currently have.

The world the learner inhabits has a huge influence on their ability to learn new skills and insights. It influences what shapes them and the priorities they have, as well as what blocks them or enables them to feel safe enough to expose themselves to new ideas or practice new behaviours.

While it's important to be aware of the reasons people have to learn, we also need to understand what incentives the different stakeholders and particularly our participants have to not learn. Mats Alvesson and André Spicer wrote an interesting book about this: *The Stupidity Paradox: The Power and Pitfalls of Functional Stupidity at Work.* Functional Stupidity is defined by them as "an organised attempt to stop people from thinking seriously about what they do at work." There is even a proverb that says that it's difficult to get someone to understand something when their salary depends on them not understanding it.[8] Kodak is a great example of this. They pioneered digital photography technology, but then abandoned it because their business was built around producing, selling

---

[8] Upton Sinclair wrote this in "I, Candidate for Governor: And How I got Licked (1935).

and developing rolls of film.

This dilemma is not exclusive to big multinational businesses. A pupil might not be motivated to do well in school, because their primary needs of being respected by their peers and parents might be earned in other ways, such as loyalty or their athletic achievements. A manager, who is evaluated on short-term business results, might not be open to learn ways to build long-term positive relations with her team members, for fear of not meeting her metrics. If you're stuck in a *"bullshit job"*[9] i.e. if your job is mainly about making your superiors feel important, acting aggressively on behalf of your employers, ameliorating preventable problems, or dealing with pointless paperwork or creating extra work for others without adding actual value – well, in this case, you might not be very motivated to get better at that job, right?

At school, I was never a very good student, particularly when it came to math, biology or any other subject that required me to memorise facts. I think the reason was that I never understood why it would or should be desirable to be able to calculate the shape a curve might take on a graph. My teacher, unfortunately, was also not really able to explain this to me (or I just wasn't paying attention - which is entirely possible).

I ended up studying just enough to get by and not fail the subject so that I could get my A-levels and enter university. My investment of time and effort was purely driven by the need to achieve a certain result, not by an intrinsic interest in the actual subject matter.

Now, almost 20 years later, it really pains me that I have a very limited understanding of how the physical world works and I try to make up for this by listening to science-podcasts and watching

---

[9] See more on this in David Graeber's book called, well, *Bullshit Jobs: A Theory*.

Neil DeGrasse-Tyson (Astrophysics) and Robert Sopolsky (Behavioural Neuroscience) videos on YouTube.

You could take a moment now to reflect on your own experiences with being motivated to learn something[10] What motivated you in the past to learn the things you now know? What are you currently learning about and why? Are there things you currently learn about that are purely driven by an intrinsic curiosity or, dare I say, passion? Are there things you're not too keen spending time on, but you have to, in order to get something else that you want? Why, for example, are you reading this book? What does it serve you and how does it fit into your world and the ambitions, pressures or other circumstances that shape your life?

Once I was at university I did really well because I knew why I was there. I could choose most of the seminars and lectures that I attended, I knew what I wanted to do with the increased knowledge that I was hoping to get out of my time there, and the material offered corresponded to an interest and curiosity that I already had. I studied Intercultural Communication and Adult Education - both subjects that I was intensely interested in due to my involvement in international youth work and plans to become a professional intercultural trainer.

It is crucial to understand why people may or may not be open to learning a new skill, fact, or way of seeing the world. We also need to respect when the individuals we work with are not open to learning what we have set out to teach. Only when

[10] I'm sometimes annoyed when reading a book and the author tells me to stop reading and think about something. I hardly ever do. So, you know - I'm not the boss of you. Feel free to ignore this and read on. It's up to you. You're the boss here

we accept their resistance as a logical position in their world and become interested and curious about that world, can we really empathise with their positions.

If we understand what people are curious and passionate about, we can use that avenue into their brain and deliver new ideas. A group of delinquent youth might not be overtly interested in developing project management skills, empathy or an ability to communicate with formal stakeholders. They might, however, be interested in setting up a skate-park, a band practice room or record an album in a professional studio. A skilled youth-worker can use that drive and passion and address all these other competences as a *by-product* of the way towards that stated goal. It's an approach called *Project-Based Learning*.

In the end, there may be a skate-park, but on the path there the youth group had to write funding applications, prepare and run a PR campaign, influence decision makers, calculate a budget and persevere in seeing the project through. For the youth, the skills they have gained along the way may be a by-product of finally having their skate-park. For the youth-worker, the skate-park may be the by-product of the journey that has allowed their participants to develop a bunch of crucial competences.

A skilled learning-facilitator will be able to connect those stated needs with the ones their participants don't know they have, but which might be quite fundamental in reaching their stated goals.

This approach doesn't just work with delinquent youth, obviously. I've found, for example, that trainings for trainers work best when the participants have an actual training to prepare and deliver. Learners in a feedback training pay a lot more attention when they are actually going to have a performance appraisal session after the training.

Some good questions to ask yourself regarding stakeholders:

- Who are the persons or entities that are touched by the learning event?

- What do they care about? What is important for them? What is their mission, their reason d'être, their idea about who they are and what they stand for?

- What will make investing time, attention or other resources into the learning event more attractive for the stakeholders?

- What do these different stakeholders need to feel during and after the learning event?

- What do these different stakeholders need to have in their hands before, during and after the learning event so that they feel seen and appreciated?

- What barriers does each of the stakeholders have that would prevent them from fully engaging in the learning event?

- What pressures and struggles exist in the worlds of the stakeholders that might influence their perspective onto the learning event?

Needs (Content, Results)

Now, a learning event is always about something. It's a math class, an internet-security conference, or an intercultural training. But any learning event is about so many more things than just what's in its title.

A math class is, yes, about math. But if it's a good math class it's also about becoming more capable of thinking abstractly about the world, becoming confident and feeling a sense of self-efficacy. A math-class has the potential to be about strengthening the community in the classroom and developing trusting, caring and mutually supportive relationships between students.

An intercultural training is, yes, about the influence of culture and different theories, case-studies and techniques that can help learners communicate in diverse contexts. But an intercultural training is also about challenging perspectives; it's about self-reflection, curiosity, humility and authentic interest in others.

Any learning event is about many different things at once and chances are, that for each stakeholder, the learning event might be about something different.

Let's take a conference, for example. Maybe its title is "The Future of Work is Human". It's organised by a non-profit organisation, it's paid for by sponsors and the attendants' participation fees. The attendants are all professionals who are working in their day job as managers and engineers. Some had their participation fee paid for by their employers, others have simply been allowed to not show up at work that day, but they had to pay the participation fee out of their own pockets. The speakers are all business leaders who are running their business outside the mainstream mechanistic ways of management. There are also some researchers and consultants who share good practice or offer workshops around communication skills and new management paradigms.

What is this conference about from each perspective?

For the organiser, the conference is about furthering their mission of promoting human centric organisational designs and management approaches. It's also about making money and increasing the organisation's capital that it can reinvest into publications, marketing materials, etc. And organising the conference might also be about positioning itself as a centre of excellence and as a resource for those curious in cutting edge management.

For sponsors, this conference might be about the attendants as a target group for their employer-branding strategy. The conference, in a way, is then about themselves, what great workplaces they have and what developmental opportunities they offer to their employees.

For the attendants, the conference might actually be about the content of the talks and workshops. They may be looking for ways to be more effective, feel better about their work and the way they approach their work or learn new information and gain new insights. But it might also be about the other attendants. Attendants may be strongly interested in developing their networks, meet like-minded people and position themselves as a member of a community that shapes the future.

The content of any learning event is very tightly linked to the needs and expectations of the different stakeholders. Content, to me, is not only specific information but literally what is inside a process.

As learning facilitators, we have to treat both the explicit and implicit needs with a lot of care and seek to let them become a reality through the learning event that we're facilitating. The explicit and implicit learning needs relate directly to what then becomes explicit and implicit content.

Explicit content is what a learning event is officially about. It's what's in the title, it's in the names of the different modules, sessions, lessons or workshops. Generally, the explicit content relates to the clearly and openly expressed needs and expectations of the direct stakeholders.

A youth exchange, for example, might be about "Exploring Diversity through Music" because the funder, let's say the European Commission, needs it to be about diversity in order to accomplish its mandate; and the organisation is a youth orchestra and the participants are all young musicians, so they need it to be explicitly about music in order to spark their interest.

A corporate training might be about "Agility and Speed" because the executive team has decided that the Agile transformation of the IT department is going too slowly.

A leadership retreat might be about "Authentic Authority" because the members of the management team must actively influence senior leaders outside their official range of authority.

Explicit content is very important because it calms everyone down. Not having the needs towards an event or project addressed can be a deal breaker for some. You don't sponsor an event that you're not happy to be associated with, you don't want to participate in something that is not about something you're interested in, and you won't send your best people to a conference that isn't about the topics you have identified as crucial to your organisation.

However, it's easy to fall into the trap that the explicit content is all that matters. Because that is not the case. If not addressed consciously, the quieter needs have a tendency to wiggle to the surface and influence the behaviour of the different stakeholders. If addressing the explicit needs of everyone means that they calm down and buy-in to the event, addressing the implicit needs means keeping everyone focused because they feel secure enough in the process because their needs are being cared for.

If you're anything like me you enjoy meeting new people and building your network, but you're uncomfortable attending events that are explicitly about networking. However, when I attend an event that is about something other than networking, I actively seek out opportunities to talk to and meet other people that do interesting stuff and are knowledgeable about things I'm interested in.

You might empathise with that.

When a student is disrupting the class with know-it-all comments and critiques at every point you're making, chances are that the classroom is, for this person, about positioning themselves as an intelligent person in front of their classmates (or themselves).

A strategy workshop might be for many of those attending a space where they can voice their frustrations with the directions of upper-management and feel like they are not alone with their needs. A school dropout might really need to have a space and experience where they are successful and competent to rebuild belief in themselves, but they may not voluntarily go to a workshop that is explicitly about self-development and confidence.

Implicit content is powerful, as it's mainly transported by how you do something, not what you talk about. By addressing the implicit needs of your participants in this way, we can show that we care, that we *see them* and that we're here for them. Through that, we earn their trust and their attention.

This brings up, of course, the question of whose needs we, as learning facilitators, are most loyal to in the case of conflicts or diverging priorities.

My stance is that my primary allegiance is always with the learners. This might require me then to negotiate the content with other stakeholders, who, while not being present at the learning event itself, have a great interest in its outcomes. With great clients and partners, this can be a very open, honest and fruitful discussion and negotiation. Sometimes it takes more time and sometimes you need to be a bit, well, stealthy, to make sure your learners are developing and growing in the best possible ways.

Questions worth asking here regarding needs and content:

- What does your learning event need to be about explicitly in order to make it attractive for all your stakeholders?

- How do you balance and spread out different content elements so that they have the time and space they need?

- What is the *nature* of each content element - is it best approached by reading, listening, watching, experiencing, discussing?

- What implicit needs do you need to translate to implicit content elements? What will you cover not by explicitly addressing them, but by *how* you will address them?

Context

We've looked at the different intangible influences that will impact our learning event; the expectations, needs and wishes of all those people and entities that are touched by what we're doing.

Now let's look at the physical environment.

Where we are, the time of the day, who else is there and how we relate to each other, how much time we have available to spend with each other - all that greatly influences what we pay attention to, what we can absorb and what is relevant to us.

The word *limitation* has a bad reputation, but in terms of creativity it's really important.

If learning facilitators had all the time in the world, access to every expert, every material, every space or piece of equipment, we'd have absolutely no idea what to do.

I know I wouldn't.

Luckily, when we are tasked with facilitating learning, the setting within which we find ourselves always has limitations. And by exploring it, we can exploit the potential of what we have at our disposal to the fullest. By understanding as much as we can the boundaries of and external influences onto the context, we can be more creative in finding opportunities. We can also see which of those limitations are massageable so that they can relax and become an opportunity.

Do we have a week, a day or a whole university semester, but only 1.5 hours each week?

Do we have 6 participants, or 300?

Do we have an imbalance of power and hierarchy in the group?

Does everyone already know each other well, or are they all strangers?

Think about how you can sort these factors and what kind of influence you have over them. How are you going to spend your energy in relation to this context? What can you attempt to change and how much time and energy will it cost you? What factors do you have to accept and work with? How can you be creative in using the environment you have?

It also matters greatly in which educational context we are. The formal education system, schools and universities, have certain characteristics that are beneficial to facilitating learning. Learners tend to spend a lot of time, years really, in these institutions and can build deep and long-lasting learning partnerships with teachers and professors. The diplomas often serve as door openers to other opportunities down the line and the educators are typically very well trained in both the subject as well as pedagogy.

Other features make it hard to really establish a supportive learning environment, such as the lack of free choice to engage with a subject, the group dynamics in the learning groups and the very distinct power-relationship between pupils and teachers along with the one-sided power of evaluating the learning progress.

Non-Formal Education (facilitated learning processes that don't end in diplomas) also have many things going for them in their favour, such as the voluntary participation and typically very interactive, playful and fun methodological approach. Organisations often rely on volunteers to implement the activities or they only reach those participants who have the time or support of their families to participate in the activities the organisations offer.

Finally, *incidental learning*, the learning that just happens in a non-facilitated way, shouldn't be disregarded at all when it comes to planning our learning events.

Let's look at the three categories of _people_, _space_ and _time_ as the main contextual domains that shape our learning events.

People

More often than not, learning is a social event. People learn with and through other people. That is particularly true in *organized* learning contexts. There is a learning facilitator of some sort there. And if it's not coaching, chances are there are others in the room who are also engaged in the process of learning. The people in their immediate surroundings have a huge impact on how easy it is for the participants to learn or how they might be inhibited. Very often, the other people in the room might be a big source of learning. The effectiveness of the learning event can stand and fall with the social dynamic in the room.

Let's have a look at some factors that can shape the effectiveness of our learning event in subtle or not so subtle ways.

Existing Social Bonds

Learning requires vulnerability, which humans have a hard time accepting when they don't feel physically and psychologically safe. I've briefly touched on the concept of psychological safety, which is defined by Edmondson as a "taken-for-granted belief about how others will respond when you ask a question, seek feedback, admit a mistake or propose a possibly wacky idea."[11] People who work together and who trust and respect each other will ideally develop psychological safety over time.

There is some great research around this, mainly from Edmondson, but also coming out of Google[12] and other organisations. When we're planning a learning event, we need to know how well the individual members of the group already know each other, not just as colleagues, but as people. When we deal with a group that meets each other for the first time, we need to plan for time to build trust and shared expectations through common experiences in the group. This can help everyone bond and feel more secure to open up to one another.

Depending on how deep, intense and personal the learning event needs to be in order to achieve its aims, the more time you may have to invest in this. You'll have a very different starting point if you're working with a leadership team or the entire department of a company, where everyone works with each other every day. A conference where the topic of the event might be interesting for everyone, but where there are no previous relationships (good and bad) will have a group dynamic that has been severely impacted by that. In fact, the lack of knowledge of each other is the main influence on the group dynamic at that point and needs to be consciously dealt with.

---

[11] Edmondson goes into much more detail in the book Teaming, which I highly recommend.

[12] You might want to check out their projects Oxygen and particularly Aristotle.

Questions to consider here regarding existing social bonds:

- How well do the people in the room know each other?

- Are there sub-groups that already know each other, does the whole group know each other, does no-one know anyone else?

- How much time do you have available to spend on building a coherent group?

- To what degree is a strong group bond and a high degree of psychological safety important to achieve the learning goals?

Hierarchy

Social groups have hierarchies - both formal and informal. When you work with a team and you have their boss in the room - certain things will not be talked about as openly as they would be were the boss not in the room. There may be domain experts and people with a significant amount of experience and the informal authority that comes with that reputation. These factors exist and we can either ignore them or deal with them directly.

Ignoring them does not mean, of course, that their influence becomes less pronounced, so I'd recommend addressing them purposefully.

To give you an example, at a company retreat I facilitated, we planned to hold so-called *"fuck up talks"*[13] near the beginning of the event to establish the sense of urgency for the deliberations that were to follow and to set an example for the openness we needed to achieve. Because we had every member of the company in the room, I asked the co-founder to be the first to get up and share a story of a recent personal failure in his business. We needed to make sure that he would role model the honesty, vulnerability and positive attitude to failure that we were trying to establish more in his company for everyone that was to follow.

As we had found out in the pre-retreat interviews, a lot of people were reluctant to take responsibility or admit to mistakes

---

[13]An idea based on the popular "Fuck-Up Night" events. As the organisation behind this describes on their website: "Fuckup Nights is a global movement and event series that shares stories of professional failure. Each month, in events across the globe, three to four people to get up in front of a room full of strangers to share their own professional failures." The goal of these events is to provide a counter-narrative to the never-failing business geniuses that preach on conference stages, but to show-case the reality of doing something in the world.

openly for fear of getting into trouble. So it was crucial that we used the influence of hierarchy to set an example and take down a barrier that had prevented honest conversations before the retreat.

During the pre-interviews I had asked a few other people to prepare and share some *"fuck up talks"* as well. After they had spoken, others in the group volunteered to share their stories too. This programme component that we had previously been a bit concerned about turned out to be a great catalyst for the openness and trust that we needed to design a good path forward for this company.

Questions to consider here regarding hierarchy:

- Are there formal or informal hierarchical differences in the room?

- In what ways might those differences influence the ability of different members of the group to express themselves and their vulnerabilities?

- How can you work with the hierarchies in the room to create space, open communication channels and take down barriers for expression?

Language

Most learning events are happening in the same language, but not all. If you have a multilingual event, considering language becomes an important factor. When do you need interpretation? Will you use simultaneous, whisper, or consecutive interpretations? When do you allow for mother-tongue working groups? When do you need groups to split up beyond their language comfort zone and make it work by themselves?

You also might need to consider language from a fluency point of view. Does everyone in the group have the same comfort with the same vocabulary? Are there technical terms, jargon or definitions that need to be addressed or given space to be clarified?

In one seminar around LGBTQ issues, I was involved with the team that decided to give everyone space to address what pronoun they would like to be addressed with. Language is a powerful tool of inclusion (and exclusion), so it is important to address it consciously.

Questions to consider here regarding language:

- Does everyone in the room speak the same *language*?

- In which ways are language use and hierarchy linked? What tools can you use to break those links or use them to increase inclusiveness and psychological safety?

- How does language influence the timing of your event? Will you need time for interpretation, translations, native-language groups, etc.?

Group size

Finally, the group size obviously has a huge impact on how you structure and run the learning event. With 4 participants, learning facilitators have a completely different dynamic to work with than 14, 40 or 400. Bigger groups generally mean more time-investment for crowd-control. Everything simply takes a lot longer with a large group: moving them, getting them to be quiet, getting everyone to understand the instructions for an exercise, getting them back from the coffee breaks, etc.

Small groups are a completely different beast. You can't break up into smaller working groups that discuss questions for a while among themselves, you need to be with them non-stop. Interactive elements might go a lot quicker than in smaller groups and some experiential exercises might not work at all.

It's safe to say that the group size has a huge influence on the types of processes you can effectively do and it needs to be considered carefully.

Questions to consider here considering group size:

- How big is your group and what implications does this have for your process?

- Will you need to work with small groups a lot to allow each individual to express themselves?

- How does the group size influence how quickly the group can *move* from one programme element to the next, both physically and mentally?

- Will you need co-facilitators? Will you need to involve participants in being co-facilitators of small groups?

Physical Environment

It's rare that participants in a learning event might feel physically unsafe. Nonetheless, this is a really important first step to be aware about. If learners don't feel physically safe, they're not going to learn anything. A large part of the brain's energy will be directed at survival and that's not going to include nuanced and reflected thought.

Assuming that we're, hopefully, not working in a war-zone, a class-room where physical punishments are the norm, or a summer camp with a bunch of poisonous animals around, the importance of physical safety is much more often connected to the availability of good food and a warm and comfortable environment.

It is absolutely true that learning events with good, healthy food and lots of natural light are more effective. If you've ever worked in a windowless room with heavy food and bad coffee, you already know how much harder everything gets.

The room, where it happens

Rooms are built for a purpose and in each detail of their design you can see the decisions that led to them (and who they're trying to please). University lecturing halls are designed to give a large group of people a good line of view to a single person up front, as well as the visuals they are showing on a screen or board.

Conference rooms in hotels are designed to be transformable into a large array of shapes and styles – from a festive dinner, to a board-meeting, to a conference, to a concert or a training course. This means that they have to compromise in optimizing for any one of those things so that they can accommodate all of them.

Sometimes you're lucky enough to have a training room that was designed for exactly the kind of thing you want to do there, but more often than not, we have to adjust and accommodate.

If you have a choice, opt for rooms that have mobile furniture, so that for each moment of the learning event, you can rearrange the room to suit your needs perfectly. Natural light is always better than strong white light. And access to an outdoor space is always better than being locked up and surrounded by smoke and skyscrapers.

The wider environment

Any learning event has a relationship with its larger environment. Most have a relation of mutual ignorance (still a relationship). Some learning events are either disrupted by or disruptive to their environment (or both), while some learning events use the environment they are placed in fully and with purpose.

If you are located in a beautiful hotel in the countryside with access to a forest, you can use the trees and the quiet of the landscape. If you are in a training room, inside the office of the company you're working with, you can use the proximity to the colleagues and peers. If you are in a school, you can use the fact that you have all these kids for such a long period of time.

Some questions to consider here regarding the physical environment:

- What possibilities lie in your physical environment that can enhance the learning process?

- What spaces encourage the type of activities you want to do and which hinder them?

- To what degree can and should you change the setting to support your learning process better?

- How can you enable different forms of activity - movement, solitary reflection, group work, having the whole group together, formal and informal moments, etc.?

Time

There is, of course, a big difference if you have a group of 100 for half a day, a group of 5 for 5 days or a group of 25 for 3 months, but only for 1.5 hours per week.

The longer the learning journey is spread out over time, the higher the amount of world that is going to interfere in your process. However, the shorter the learning event is, the less likely it is that you can go deep enough into the topic or build enough experience to make sure you have the intended transformative impact.

That is because everything needs time. Building trusting relationships with your co-learners takes time. Exploring a new topic takes time. Practicing new skills take time. But also having a family and hobbies and just simply a life outside the learning event – it all takes time. When planning a learning event, we need to have a holistic view over all the demands for our learner's time and to what else they need to pay attention to outside of what we have to offer them.

Questions to consider here regarding time:

- How much time of your participants do you have access to?

- What other things might your participants need or want to spend time on that have nothing to do with your learning event (i.e. family, hobbies, work, etc.)?

- How long do the activities that you're planning last and to what degree do you need to build in flexibility and adaptability to your process?

- Which time-slots are non-negotiable (meal times, start and finish times, guest speakers, etc.) and which moments are highly flexible?

So, here we are.

We understand the world our learners are embedded in and all the forces that touch our learning events.

We've explored the needs and expectations of the different stakeholders and have taken them seriously.

We've mapped out the needs of the different stakeholders to specific content elements, both explicitly and implicitly.

We looked long and hard at the environment, the setting, the time and the composition of the group.

Essentially, we know who we're dealing with, where we are and where we want to go.

Now it's time to plan our journey.

It's time to come up with the story that'll get us to our destination.

3

The learning flow - building the story

Phase I: Purposeful Departure   p. 70

Phase II: Exploration   p. 74

Phase III: Transformative
Integration   p. 76

PART III: The learning flow - building the story

Once we have a clear understanding of the world our learning event is set within, about the limitations we have and what needs and expectations are directed towards us, we can get to building the Learner's Journey.

Dan Harmon's Story Circle has eight steps. Those same steps are perfect as design principles for developing learning events as well.

I'm further breaking those eight steps down into three phases: *Purposeful Departure, Exploration*, and *Transformative Integration*. This is done to help make it easier to structure the learning event later on.

To start things off, let's have a look at each of the points, just shortly. After that, we'll go much more in depth into each of them.

Phase I: Purposeful Departure

Protagonist

PROTAGONIST

The protagonist of any learning event is the learner and not the learning facilitator. This is so crucially important that I can't stress it enough. Also because it's just so damn easy to forget, when we're standing there on the stage in front of the room, and we get to explain something we're excited about.

However, when creating a learning journey we need to think of it from the perspective of the learner and design specific moments so that the individuals, as well as the group, can realise themselves as the protagonists of the adventure they are about to embark on. By understanding the protagonist(s), we can also understand their world, what motivates them, what they fear and what their ambitions are.

Steve Jobs is attributed with saying "Good design is not how it looks like, it's how it works." In recent times a shift in design has gone from just making stuff look nice to "User Experience Design" – considering the whole experience of using something that is beyond the aesthetics of it.

In that same sense, learning facilitators are not designing a curriculum - we're designing a learning experience. And we just can't do that without deeply understanding within whom that experience is going to take place and letting them constantly feel that what we're doing is for them.

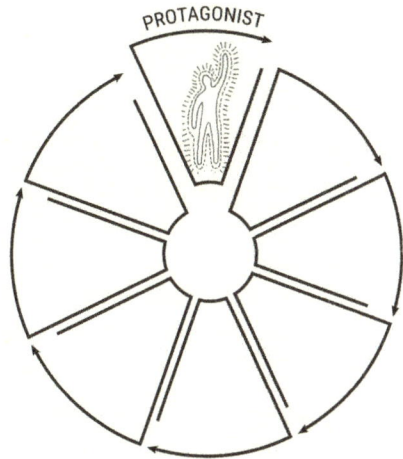

Have a *Need*

Learning something new and leaving the comfort zone is hard. In order to do it, the learners need to be sure that it's really necessary to go into the unknown. In this step of the learning journey, the gap between how things are and how they should be needs to be highlighted. It needs to become clear for the participants that they have to go into the unknown if they want the better version of reality to be the one they can inhabit.

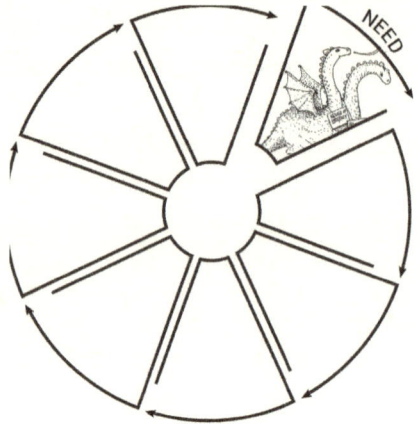

People only go into the unknown if it's clear that *here* is no longer good enough and that beyond the unknown is a life that is much better. Thomas Keller, a famous chef, has a sign in his kitchens that says *Sense of Urgency* because that's the spirit he wants to feel as the chefs are preparing super delicate food. We might not need to go this far with our learners even though a *sense of urgency* will certainly be a good motivator. But we can't reasonably expect our participants to explore the unknown without a *sense of purpose*.

And then *Go*.

This is when the learners exit the comfort zone and the real adventure starts. When, as facilitators of the learning path, we have done our work well in establishing *The Protagonists* and *Need* steps, the participants will now have a strong and intrinsic motivation to go into the unknown and discover something new. As with any departure, the emotional aspect of it is often the one that makes it hard, not the logistics or even the length that it takes. Our task as learning facilitators is to make this departure possible.

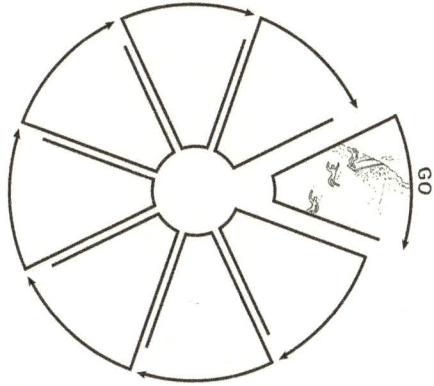

Phase II: Exploration

The *Search* begins.

In the *Search* phase, participants need to have the chance to *fail interestingly*; to question what they know, try again, fail, learn from it and try again. Participants might train new skills that they're uncomfortable with or expose themselves to new information so that they might have a better understanding of parts of the world that were previously a mystery to them. It's here that they explore and challenge themselves. The higher the sense of urgency around acquiring the skills and knowledge to undertake this paradigm shift, the more serious they'll be about this.

They *Find* something new.

The *Find* step is hard, maybe even impossible, to control by a learning facilitator, as each participant might find something different as they *Search*. They also might end up not finding that one insight,

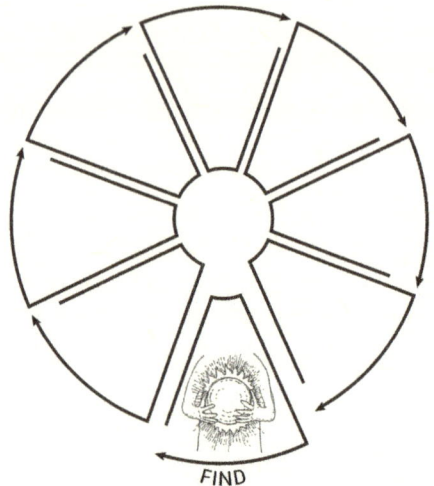

FIND

perspective or question that they were looking for (or that was looking for them), but instead find something they didn't expect.

This happens all the time. Participants might learn about the thing that you've promised to teach them but the main AHA moment is about something else, maybe something deeper, maybe about something more implicit.

Complicating it even further: sometimes this stage doesn't even happen inside the classroom.

Take it.

In the *Take* step, the participants transform what they have found and make it theirs. They integrate the new skill/knowledge/ perspective into their own world and their internal map of the world. But these new insights are only useful and can only enrich and change the protagonist's world. To bring change into the known world, a new insight needs to really have become part of who the learners are now. That requires purpose and focus, as much as in any other step. If we teach someone a new skill, but we do not prepare them in any way to actually use that skill in their normal context, the chances that this skill will evaporate are extremely high.

Phase III: Transformative Integration

They Return into the known.

In this phase, participants either literally return into their contexts or they plan their return. We think about how to integrate the new knowledge into the contexts and realities where participants are from and where they will apply what they have learned in our learning event. This can be a difficult step for us as learning facilitators, because we have to let go and trust that the learners are strong enough to independently and confidently bring what they have learned and integrate it into their world.

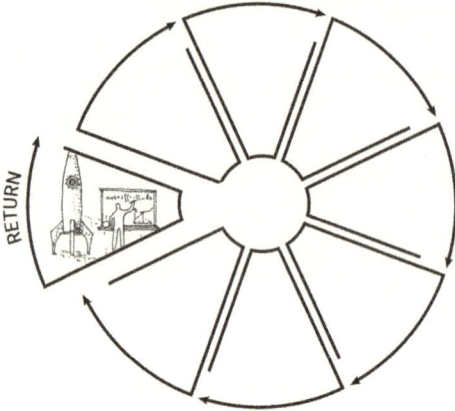

Having changed and bringing *Change*.

In order for the new insights, skills and perspectives to become applicable and actually contribute an improvement to the participants' worlds, the aspect of change needs to be directly addressed on two dimensions. On the one hand, we need to facilitate the protagonists realisation of how they have changed personally (even if only a little bit) and what this change means for their environment. On the other hand, we need to provide the time and space to actively think about how their new insights might change their contexts and how they will be agents of that change.

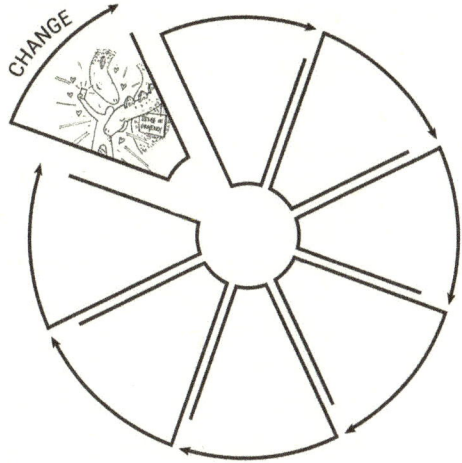

Makes sense? Now let's look at each step in more detail.

Phase I: Purposeful Departure

THE PROTAGONISTS - "I see you"

How this works in the stories we know

Every good story is about someone. Sure, there are other characters around them that are meaningful and important and who go through different levels of transformation, but there's often one core character to each story. The recent *Star Wars* movies are about Rey and how she figures out who she is and what her destiny is. Frodo is the main character of *The Lord of the Rings*. Hamlet is the main character of, wait for it, *Hamlet*. And Harry Potter, OK...joke's getting old.

Sometimes, however, there is not one person that is the protagonist, but there is a group who each individually go through a process of transformation, but they're also together on a journey and support each other. *Friends*, *The Avengers*, *Guardians of the Galaxy* or the cast of *Love Actually* are great examples of this genre.

Some stories bring you right to the protagonist in the first sentence. Take Franz Kafka's opening line to his short story "Metamorphosis": "As Gregor Samsa awoke one morning from uneasy dreams he found himself transformed in his bed into a gigantic insect."

Establishing the main character in a fictional story is really important, because the protagonist can only really do their job (keeping readers engaged for hours on end, or movie viewers in their seats for the whole running time), when the audience identifies with them.

In a fictional story, writers and filmmakers do this by showing the protagonist. Simple as that. The author reveals the protagonist doing something and boom, we're them until someone more relatable comes along. Most protagonists in fictional stories are a combination of some characteristics that we can relate to – they're both someone we are and someone we'd like to be.

How we can use that in the learning events we create

When we want to support our participants in being the hero of their own transformative journey, our task is not so much to establish them as the protagonist. They are already the protagonist of their own life and hopefully our learning event will fit snugly in the storyline that's been running before they arrived at our door.

No, our task is avoiding the things we could do that would make them feel like they're not the protagonist. And that's easier said than done.

How many learning events start with passivity? Too many in my experience. Participants come in and sit down and it takes hours until they get to talk and express themselves. All this shows that the learning event is not *about* them. They're merely the audience, the consumers.

In many circumstances our goal might be that we aim to establish the group of participants as a collective of protagonists - think *Friends*, *Avengers*, etc. Each person is on their own journey but the group is there to support one another, and the group as such is the context for achieving the personal learning needs. This will often be the case in learning events such as seminars or training courses, conferences or workshops where the participants will not be working in that same constellation with each other again.

Then we can also think of the group as a protagonist. This approach works well in settings where an entire team, department or even company is participating in a learning event together, such as retreats, strategy workshops or team-coaching sessions.

Instead of stressing how important this step is, let's consider what happens if this step doesn't get enough attention.

Imagine you are attending a training course and NOT thinking "This is about me and my learning and growth," but instead you have the feeling that you being there is irrelevant, maybe even annoying. I know of teachers and lecturers who have openly stated (not to their students, but to their peers) that they don't really like their students. I've sat through presentations and lectures where I had the very distinct feeling that the person speaking was not there to be of service to my learning process, but that I was replaceable and that it was really only about having a stage and hearing their voice or the fact that this was their job, which was driving the presentation. It's hard to pay attention in such circumstances.

In films or books, the protagonist gets introduced fairly quickly, often within the first few minutes of engaging with the material. The easiest, fastest and stickiest way to introduce the hero of the story is to show them first. We should do the same in learning events: create the space for our participants to show themselves first.

In the class or training room, most participants that interrupt or monopolise the space do so because they feel like they haven't been seen – either by the learning facilitator or by their peers. They might feel that their previous experiences and insights are being ignored even though they provide such an important context to understanding where they are starting from.

A conference that doesn't allow the group of participants to experience themselves as the focus of the event will involve themselves less to the process. A training course that doesn't start with the participants in the room, that doesn't include their experiences and current perspectives onto the challenges ahead - that course will need to spend a lot of time later bringing the participants back into the process, if that is even still a possibility.

Most participants that are internally checked-out and don't pay attention do so because they feel that the content has nothing to do with them. Who can blame them then for checking out? As the facilitators of their learning process we're asking them to pay attention, and that willingness is a lot easier if we have already been paying our attention to them.

OK, that was a bit negative.

Let's turn our attention from what we should probably avoid doing to how to actually create this learner-centric environment right from the start. It is absolutely crucial to begin every learning journey with a good look at the participants who are in the room and to truly acknowledge who they are and what experiences they already have in relation to the content of the training or conference.

We can do this by either asking them directly, either on the phone or in person. I do this routinely before highly customised retreats or workshops and it's super useful.

If we don't have access to the learners beforehand, we can do our best to work with what we have: empathy, data, secondary information such as articles, videos or other media. We should invest time in the beginning of each learning event for participants to introduce themselves with more than their name. By doing something together, by showing themselves and what they bring, participants can be seen, heard and express very clearly who they are and what they bring.

We might also want to spend some time thinking about how we can go from a *This is Me* to a *This is Us* feeling and perception within the participant's group. This will allow the opportunity to turn the group of individuals into a fellowship that goes onto a journey of discovery and mutual support together.

The source of the learning becomes exponentially bigger as participants don't only receive learning support from whoever is officially in charge of the learning but from their peers as well. And by becoming a source of learning to their peers, what they know and understand deepens as they explain it to their fellow learners.

Sabuwona is a greeting in the language of the Zulu. It's used as *hello*, but it means so much more. Literally translated, it means *I see you*. In the movie Avatar, the way the Na'vi express that they love someone is by saying *I see you*. It means *I see your personality*; *I see your humanity*; *I see your dignity*; *I respect you as who you are*; *I see your whole you*.

Wow, what a way to be treated.

Imagine if we could greet our participants into the learning journey with us in this spirit - by seeing them. By striving to understand their world and their place in it. By respecting their desires, their fears and their obstacles to learning the things we have prepared for them. Because only by seeing the person we're about to accompany on a learning journey as who they are; by not looking down at or up to them, but by meeting them with authentic interest and, yes, I'll say it, love, can we design a programme, curriculum or developmental path that makes sense for them and only them.

So how can we achieve this? Here are a few ways I have approached this in the past:

In a training for facilitators, the team I was a part of decided to start the training course with a Flip-Chart in the middle of the training room that simply said: "Dear Facilitators, facilitate." It went on to ask the group to divide into five smaller groups, each group taking charge of facilitating a part of the welcome session – from exploring and explaining the programme, to learning each other's names, to coming up with a contract for the group. The symbolism of the moment was palpable. We essentially said that this was our training course, together. We asked them to trust us and we showed that we trusted them. The first experience the participants of this training course made was of being active, of taking ownership and responsibility for their own learning and that of their peers. It was really nice.

During a conference I was co-organising, we gave each person a name-tag at registration. But it was empty with just a few questions: How do you want to be addressed? Where are you a local? What do you love to talk about? As participants filled this in, they looked at each other's name tags and started talking to each other about their answers. They found like-minded people and learned from each other and before the first official session had even started, the participants were already talking about the conference topic. They were engaged and important to each other.

Regularly, when I run intercultural trainings, I start with an exercise called *Magic Stick*.[14] The group of participants is given the task of balancing a stick together on their index fingers and laying the stick on the floor. However, what happens is that the stick goes up for reasons too complicated to describe here. What's interesting is how people react – with laughter, or disengagement, with blaming or frustrations. We later debrief the exercise to make sense of all of these reactions and compare

---

[14] It's also known as *Helium Stick*.

them to how our minds and bodies react when our normalcy-expectations are violated in other contexts that don't involve a stick that won't go down. This exercise also helps in putting participants front and centre right from the get-go. They have been in the centre, they have done something that is being talked about and their personal experiences become the main vehicle of speaking about the subject of the training.

Questions to consider regarding The Protagonists stage:

- How can I create an experience right in the beginning that allows participants to be actors, creators and the content of the learning event itself?

- What do I want my participants to see, feel and experience within the first hours of the learning event?

- What emotions, experiences and thoughts do I want to provoke in the participants that are theirs and remain with them as a resource for learning throughout?

- What do the participants need to see, feel or experience to know that *this is about me*?

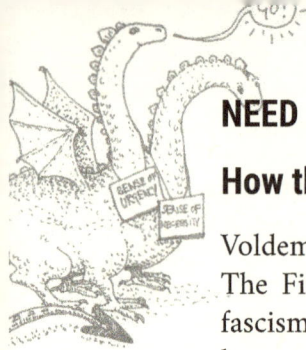

NEED - "The Gap"

How this works in the stories we know

Voldemort might rise to power and establish wizard-fascism. The First Order might rule the galaxy and establish space-fascism. Sauron might rule Middle-Earth and enslave every elf, human, hobbit or dwarf and establish orc-fascism.

The gap between how the world is and how it should or shouldn't be is pretty clear. And it's also pretty clear that if Frodo doesn't destroy the ring, if Harry doesn't defeat Voldemort or Rey doesn't stand up to Kylo Ren – all would be lost. There is a real sense of urgency. And it's this sense of urgency that saturates every moment of the story that is being told. Every fact, big or small, relates to this urgency.

How we can use that in the learning events we create

There is no learning without a need to do so. Learning in itself is not something that comes easily to us because learning requires change.

In most of the stories I mentioned above, there is an actual crisis to be averted. Fortunately, when it comes to learning something new, it's often not that tragic. The alternative to learning is very rarely space/wizard/orc-fascism, but something more subtle: the cost of *not* developing, growing and increasing one's potential and competence. If the participants are fairly satisfied with where they are, if their devil-you-know is not the worst devil they could imagine, they might very reasonably ask why they should go through all this effort.

So instead of pointing out how bad it might be if we don't venture out into the unknown, we might need to point out how much better it could be for our participants after having gone through the learning journey with us.

We, as humans, are afraid of (unnecessary) change. Having changed and having learned is a different story - that's great.

I'm sure that when I have this book done I'll be super happy about the things I learned as I was writing it. But right now, let me tell you, keeping the motivation up to sit down and write and think and... change, that's really hard. Millions of books remain unwritten because of it. Lots of "Uh, that could be interesting to learn more about" remains just that thought and never results in active research, reading books and interviewing experts. Because that's work.

When I was in high school, my math teacher asked if anyone had a remote-control car at home. A classmate of mine had one and he brought it to school the next day. In the lesson, we leaned a plank of wood onto the wall and drove the car up it. It was a lot of fun. We kept increasing the angle at which we drove the car up and at one point, the angle was too steep and the car fell backwards off the ramp. Our math teacher then showed us a method with which we could calculate at which angle the car would fall off. And this marks the moment when, for the first and last time, math classes were fun for me and I was fully engaged. That's because this teacher didn't give me an answer to reproduce, but a question that intrigued me along with a map towards finding the answer myself.

The same phenomenon is true for all learning events. If the main need you have towards attending a conference is to give your talk (because you need that on your CV), you'll have little attention left for learning from the other speakers. If your only reason to be at a certain training session is to write your name on the attendance list, because your boss told you to attend, your learning motivation will likely be limited to figuring out where that damn attendance list is hiding.

In the big stories, heroes rarely choose to go on their journey voluntarily. Hermione doesn't want to go fight the Death Eaters and send her parents to Australia as little as Happy Potter wants to face-off with Voldemort. They realise that they have to, because the world these villains represent is not a world Hermione or Harry are prepared to live in.

An additional challenge for us is that most people have relatively powerful internal mechanisms that prevent them from realising that they're not great at something or that it might be worth learning more about it. Unfortunately, learning requires the acceptance that we have the potential to learn more and that, in fact, the efforts of learning this will be totally worth the version of ourselves that is able to do the thing in a way we're currently not able to.

Just because people show up doesn't always mean that they have the necessary sense of urgency and relevance to give them energy to stay with it, even when it gets hard.

Just because people are there physically, doesn't mean that they have the space for the learning process mentally.

If we as learning facilitators don't show that we deserve this precious mental space, by providing pathways to solutions to actual, emotionally relevant problems they have, then we shouldn't complain if they solve more relevant problems of theirs (such as receiving immediate gratification by counting their hearts on Instagram or seeing comments to their posts on Facebook).

Facilitating learning means making it easy to learn (Facilis in Latin means easy). Sometimes the process of making it easier to learn requires us to let people experience first-hand that they are incompetent at something and that it's OK and normal. Sometimes it might require us to let people know that their peers wish they were better at communicating, time-management or delegation, or whatnot. If we provide a safe space and make sure they know that this is about them and for them, they might find it easier to accept this truth and consequently buckle up for a ride into the unknown.

The most valuable thing we can give a participant at this point is a question mark they have not had before or to amplify and acknowledge one they brought with them. Not our question mark, mind you. This is not the time for a quiz, where we show them how much they don't know stuff we know. This is about *their* question mark, based on their experience, reflection or critical inquiry.

Why do people behave this way? Why do I behave this way? What would I be able to do or understand if I knew this set of facts? How could I stop doing this and start doing that? I've seen a future that I like – how can I get there?

In previous projects, I have approached exploring and developing the needs in different ways. See if you can take these as a starting point and develop something that suits your learning event from there:

The *Magic Stick* exercise that I mentioned earlier is a really great way to combine the You with the Need because it puts question marks into the participants' heads. The first question is, why did that stick go up? But the more meaningful questions come afterwards: Why did I react the way I did? Do I always react this way unconsciously when unexpected things happen? Why did we communicate so chaotically as a group and why was I not able to solve this challenge more constructively? I'd like to think of myself as someone who is able to do this, so what do I need to learn now to become that person?

In a conference a few years ago, we decided to invite a speaker for the first afternoon that would give a *world on fire talk*. Her task was to paint a picture of urgencies, to shine a light on everything that's not working well, that's the opposite of how we'd like the world to be, that is unacceptable for good people. The room was full of people who were engaged in social work, youth work and international exchanges. Good people who do good work and who think of themselves as being on the right side of history.

The speaker we invited challenged all of those self-perceptions. She asked the question: is what you are doing enough? Are you complicit in a system that manifests an inherently unjust power structure? And she laid out a slew of facts that showed that, in fact, they might be. This rattled the participants a bit.

We followed this with an evening session of *Stories of Hope,* where we invited different activists to share their success stories, their approaches to making a positive impact in small but meaningful ways. This combination of "The world isn't as it should be" and "There are people who do amazing work" provided the necessary questions of "Is what I'm doing enough?" and "How can I learn from my peers and step up?" A powerful mix that fuelled the engagement for the following days of exchange, workshops, learning, growth and strategic thinking about the future.

At a strategic planning and evaluation retreat, I guided the participants early in the programme through a dream journey. This guided meditation brought the participants to revisit the previous project stages, re-feel their moments of pride as well as their moments of frustration. I then asked them to reimagine those frustrating moments and change them in their minds. What would they do differently now? And what do they need to do in order to be equipped with doing it differently in the future?

My questions started with *What if...?, Imagine that...?* and *What itch is still left to scratch?* I brought the participants out of the meditation with very clear ideas of what needs their focus now, what they want to change in the context they came from and what they'll need from the retreat to make that happen.

Questions to consider regarding the NEED stage:

- How can I create a safe enough environment that allows participants to admit that it might be worth investing energy into improving something?

- What first-hand experiences can I create for participants that exemplify the need to invest time and mental energy to explore a topic?

- What reflections can I stimulate in participants that allows them to clearly identify how things are and how they could be?

- How can I highlight the space after the learning as being desirable enough for participants to push through challenging moments in the learning journey?

GO - "The jump"

How this works in the stories we know

In the best stories, this is when the hero sets out. It's when Rey from *Star Wars* jumps into the Millennium Falcon with Finn and sets off to bring BB-8 to the rebel base. It's when Harry Potter boards the train to Hogwarts. It's when Moana takes the boat and leaves the island to the open sea.

At this point in the stories the hero doesn't have the answers anymore, the competences that helped get them by in the known, comfortable environment don't help anymore - the passage into darkness starts.

Anything can happen. They will discover strengths they didn't know they had, they will realise things about themselves and the world that have been in plain sight all along but not accessible, and they will suffer and yet prevail because the journey's destination is worth it.

Think of it this way - you're climbing up a 3 meter high springboard. It's clear that it's you going up there and with every step you make it clearer and clearer that it's going to be you who'll jump into the pool, no-one else. When you're on top the gap is clear. You're up there, you want to be down there, in the water.

Now, I don't know about you, but in my experience, the most interesting sensation is not necessarily the journey down. It's that split second when you make up your mind that you ARE going to jump; where you take that leap; when you think to yourself "Well, I guess I am actually going to do this." You bend your knees and you overcome that sensation in your body that tells you that it's super silly to jump from 3 meters up.

It's this crossing of the threshold that is the real thrill. It's so short, but at least for me, it's the feeling I can remember much better than the feeling of actually falling into the water. The same is true, by the way, for bungee jumping and when you take your first breath under water using scuba-diving equipment.

It's not the jump, it's the decision to jump that's the hardest and it needs a feeling of physical and psychological safety to be possible.

Think of a time you *took a leap*. What was that all about and how did it feel?

How we can use that in the learning events we create

The most important condition for the jump into the unknown in a learning context is trust. True learning requires vulnerability and that requires the belief that we're going to be fine. Participants need to know that they'll be supported, that they'll be safe, and even when we challenge them, they are not in danger. And that trust is up to us as learning facilitators to have earned before we ask the participants to join us in the discomfort of the unknown.

At this point, in great learning events, we see a change in format, a change in speed and a change in informational direction. While the next phase is very much about finding something new (through research, teaching, training, etc.) the *Go* step is the transitional phase where it has to be established what this whole endeavour is about.

Here, participants collectively and individually commit that they are ready and open to explore and discover new ideas. It's at this stage that you're either in or you're out because now the actual work really starts. It's very difficult, in the programme design for a training course, conference or university seminar to make this an observable and controllable moment. It can be done by changing the room, by literally *going* to a different place.

If the context works for this, the group might choose to make a learning contract with each other, or a buddy system can be established to make the peer-support tangible. Very often this change in the programme from preparing to go to being in the middle of exploring, learning and challenging ideas is...a coffee break.

At a conference I had worked on as the programme designer and then facilitator, we spent the first half of the first day of the official programme in a large plenary room, where the conference was recognised by dignitaries and then headlined by a powerful speaker who laid out the urgency of the topics we would tackle during the meeting.

After a lunch break, the participants literally went to different rooms, each one dedicated to a sub-topic of the conference, where they prepared ways to showcase their own expertise in those areas and what they were able to share with their peers. By changing the context, by removing ourselves from the space where the participants were the *audience* to spaces where they would be resources, creators and *givers*, we changed the dynamic and the ways participants thought of and experienced themselves.

At a training for trainers I was involved in, we prepared a Learning Journal for all participants, which we gave them in the *Go* phase. The first pages were dedicated to personal reflections and a setting of individual learning goals for the course. Participants noted what they wanted to achieve, what they wanted to specifically learn and how they planned to make use of the resources they would have at their disposal during the training.

Through this, we created the conditions for intentionality; for taking personal responsibility towards oneself. The act of writing this down, by physically manifesting it marked the *Go* in this case. By stating it clearly, if only to themselves, participants made a commitment that they would revisit again and again throughout the training.

Questions to consider regarding the Go stage:

- How *deep* is the jump I'm asking my participants to make and what symbols of support and safety do they require to enable them to make that step?

- What symbolism of change can I employ to make the transition from the known into the unknown tangible?

- How can I create the conditions for participants to take responsibility and ownership over their own jump?

- What mechanisms of physical and psychological safety can I establish to ensure learning support throughout the next challenges?

- In what ways can I use the physical space to evoke a literal departure?

Phase II: Exploration

SEARCH - "The Challenge"

How this works in the stories we know

Joseph Campbell called this phase the *The Road of Trials*, but it's also been known as *The Training Phase or Friends, Enemies and Allies*. I like *The Road of Trials* because it has the idea of challenges baked right into it.

This is the part in the stories where the protagonists have to struggle. They fight, they fail and through the failure they learn something important about themselves or about their nemesis, or both. Luke Skywalker learns that Darth Vader is his father (and loses a hand in the process), Frodo literally carries a burden, Sam carries Frodo, and Aragorn has to come to believe in himself as a king. Moana has to fight little coconuts, a giant crab and a lava monster, as well as deal with a grumpy demi-god who's a bit fragile in his masculinity because his hook isn't working well. It's all not easy. But educational.

The *Search* phase in most stories is the longest part of the story with most of the action. I mean, *The Lord of the Rings* movies manage to spend a good 90 minutes of going through the *You*, *Need* and *Go* and then roughly 10 hours of *Search*.

Joseph Campbell describes this part to be very similar to the digestive tract of our body. It takes the protagonists down and strips off all the baggage, the preconceptions, the bullshit, the fear and the illusions so that they can see themselves as who they really are and with that pure strength emerge successfully.

The *Search* phase is not necessarily a consistently happy phase, nor does it need to be all mayhem all the time. It requires moments of calmness and rest in order to get through it, as much as it requires the interesting failures that test and challenge our protagonists. It is a road of challenges with successes and failures equally distributed along the way. There is no transformation possible without the challenge. There is no possible acceptance of the challenge without the baseline trust that it'll be alright in the end.

How we can use that in the learning events we create

If we have not done a good job in working out why learning something new is necessary, then it's very likely that participants won't mobilise their curiosity, attention and care. And they are right not to do so, because it's hard work that we typically only spend when the resulting state is better than the situation we're already in.

However, if we have done a good job in earning the participants' trust, then they should willingly follow us into this darkness and challenge themselves with new information, perspectives, skills sets and abilities. Because it's worth it to them.

What's important is that in the search phase, we need strong mechanisms of input, experimentation, prototyping, physical and emotional experiences, practice, and a whole lot of feedback.

It's simply not enough to say things once and in one way only. On the one hand, people learn in different ways, obviously. On the other hand, practice is the key to mastering a new skill. On the magically appearing third hand, learning from experience is much easier, longer lasting and more meaningful. Experience is nothing else but making mistakes, examining them and trying again. Experiential learning is incredibly powerful and we need to make sure that our participants generate or refer to as much personal experience as possible to fuel their learning.

However, exclusively relying on directly generated experience in the learning event isn't always enough, of course. As Yuval

Noah Harari pointed out[15], humans are not where they are today in the food chain because they are the fastest, strongest nor most aggressive species. Our ability to learn not only from our own mistakes and achievements, but also from our grandma's and great-great-grandma's experiences allowed us to overtake the super slow process of biological evolution that all other species go through.

Once we started to write stuff down and were able to learn not only from the people we know, but from anyone that knows anything we don't – well, let's just say that it makes sense that the speed of knowledge creation and human progress has accelerated significantly after writing and publishing became a thing.

All this is to say that a little bit of input isn't a bad thing. While some contexts rely too heavily on it (schools, universities, some conferences, etc.), others vilify it too much (social work, youth work, sports, etc.). Explaining something, presenting some facts, or sharing some insights can be really useful. Especially if it helps to prepare learners for an experience, or understand why what happened in a previous exercise happened the way it did.

By going through this process of iterative learning during the Search phase, we stay close to the learners and can adapt the input to meet the insights from the feedback they have received and shape the practice phases so that that the previous input can immediately be applied, tested and integrated into the portfolio of knowledge and skills the learner has access to.

There are different ways to fail and not all of them are helpful. The sort that I tend to promote is to try and *fail interestingly*. No-one likes to feel like a failure, to be a failure or to just *not win* - it's very hard to learn from that at all. So it will

---

[15] In the already mentioned book *Sapiens*.

often be our task to make sure our participants can look at the experiences that were not up to scratch, that went wrong or simply turned out different than expected and say "Fascinating."

By creating a context that is non-judgemental and psychologically safe, we can allow our participants to step over that edge from the comfort to the stretch zone. From there, they can inch towards the border of the panic zone and enjoy the ride of failing in ways that shows them new paths forward.

Knowledge and skills are best acquired if four principles are met, according to a standard textbook on educational psychology[16]:

1. The learner needs to give the new information enough attention.

2. There is a need for a certain amount of repetition and practice.

3. The new information needs to be given sense within the already existing context of skills and knowledge that the learner already has.

4. The new and the old sets of knowledge and skills need to be integrated with each other and consolidated into a new landscape of competence that the learner now has.

The first principle is often the trickiest because we, as learning facilitators, can only indirectly control how much attention our participants are willing to give. Attention is a valuable currency, isn't it? It's not by accident that the general usage of this word is that we pay attention.

When it comes to the service-relationship between learner and learning facilitator, that's what we literally get paid with.

---

[16] *Pädagogische Psychologie* by Marcus Hasselhorn and Andreas Gold

Attention from other people is hard to earn and even harder to keep. Countless conferences, training courses or school lessons struggle with continuously earning the attention of the participants throughout the event. There's a whole world in everyone's pocket and an entire universe in everyone's imagination. And either one of those is often more interesting than what is happening in the front of the room.

So we continuously need to make sure what we have to offer makes sense in the world of the learner, that it is embedded in their context and that it responds to a need they have for themselves.

The second principle, the need for repetition, is clear. If you do something once and never again, it won't be incorporated into your inner catalogue: *stuff I can do*. On a neurological level, this is actually measurable. Hearing something new sparks an activation within a certain neural network in your brain. If you want to be able to retrieve that spontaneously later on without strong priming (reminding), you need to establish a *long-term potentiation* between those neurons, keeping the electrical charge up, basically.[17]

And you tell those neurons that their connection might be important by, well, repeatedly firing those neurons over and over. It needs to be highlighted that repetition only makes sense if there is a feedback-loop built into the repetitive practice.

To repeatedly run into a wall isn't going to teach you anything besides a deep understanding of the variety of headache pills available on the market. The repetition of practice needs to always be intersected with a critical look at one's own actions. And, who knows, there might be a door around the corner

---

[17] You will have noticed that I mentioned this earlier in the book. Repetition in practice!

worth discovering.

The third and fourth principles are all about connecting the world as it is with the world as it could be: to remain the person the learners have been in the world that they inhabited before but also progress and change.

This is the story each learner gets to tell about themselves as they leave the safety of the learning context and return to their daily lives. This story will continue once they are in the space where they are actually supposed to implement their new insights and turn them into actionable choices, behaviours or standpoints.

This is not to be taken lightly.

We all have a network of knowledge and skills and attitudes neatly laid out and arranged in our head. You can literally look at this network through neural mapping technologies. As learning happens, the little path through the meadow slowly turns into a trail, into a street, into a highway (hello, long-term potentiation), into a hyper-loop until we know what we know so deeply that we're hardly aware of the thought process.

This is great, but it also means that we can be quite immune to learning at times. The deeper and stronger old knowledge and paradigms are entrenched in our neural networks, the harder it is to incorporate a different paradigm or an insight that challenges our old conceptions of how the world works and the story of who we are in it, etc.[18] This doesn't happen by itself.

Learning something is one thing, making it sustainable and allowing it to really sink in is a whole new ball game that needs to be addressed by the learning facilitators with care.

---

[18] As is often observable when it comes to internal politics in organisations and institutions.

Particularly when we are working with a group of diverse people, who have diverse learning needs and ways of learning.

It's going to be crucial that we allow for different forms of learning in this phase. To only discuss, to only do an experiment, to only read and write, to only sit and think or watch video tutorials, is not going to be effective. A mix of all of these things is probably going to be the most effective. A specific method or module might correspond directly to some participant's learning styles. Others will just come along then, hoping that their learning preferences will be met in a later module of your learning event. Our task is to make sure their hope is not in vain.

In this area, a bunch of practical examples are probably not the most noteworthy, because there is such a richness of teaching methods out there.

During trainings for trainers, I always make sure the participants prepare and run training sessions on relevant topics for their peers, having thus a two-pronged learning experience: the actual content of the training session run by themselves or their peers and on the meta level, the way the training sessions were prepared, run and evaluated.

There are many great lectures available on YouTube and platforms such as Udemy and many others.

Resources such as Compass, the Human Rights Education Manual of the Council of Europe is an extremely good resource to find methods to cover topics ranging from discrimination, minority empowerment, active citizenship and hard human rights knowledge.

The World Cafe and Open Space are great methods to learn and experiment with ideas and perspectives.

Questions to consider regarding the Search stage:

- How can I give my participants a chance to fail interestingly?

- How can we repeat crucial information and behaviours, but in ways that are enabling reflection and progress?

- What safe spaces, environments or moments can I build into the programme that allow participants to feel supported?

- How can I adjust the programme to different levels of challenge, based on diverse participant needs?

- Is the input I'm offering related to where my participants are coming from and where they are going?

FIND - "The Encounter"

How this works in the stories we know

It's when Harry Potter understands (spoiler alert!) that for Voldemort to be killed, he must die as and it's through this insight he prevails. It's when Rey picks up the Laser-Sword in *The Force Awakens* and accepts that she is special, different and that she can fight Kylo Ren and win. It's when Aragorn picks up the sword Anduril and reveals himself to Sauron as the king who has returned. It's when Moana dives into the sea to pick up the heart of Te Fiti. It's when Julia Roberts is in the book-shop as just a girl, standing in front of a boy, asking him to love her.

Dan Harmon describes this moment as *weightless*, when everything is possible. Whatever it is, it's certainly a turning point. It's the climax. The protagonist has been tumbling down, challenged and searching. They have learned new things about themselves and the world and now suddenly it's "Ahhh, now I get it!"

The powerful star is now a girl with a heartache, the hero realises that what she has seen before as her biggest weakness is actually her biggest strength. It's a moment of vulnerability, but also strength.

It's what we wait for in every story we witness.

How we can use that in the learning events we create

Do you remember the last time something clicked and you suddenly got something?

Like when you've been working for a long time to learn how to play a piece of music on the piano and you've been focused on the technique, where to put your fingers when, etc. And now your fingers know the piece and you can just play and suddenly you realise that you're not just pressing keys to make sounds, but you're expressing something, you're saying something through the music and it's wow.

It's when you learn how to juggle and the balls just fly and you can start to feel like you're actually in control.

I witnessed such a moment at a company retreat. The CEO and co-founder told me in an astonished-but-glad-voice that he had thought the retreat would be all about his team learning something but he was realising that it was him. He had the biggest steps to take and the hardest changes to own so that his team had the space for development. I could see the paradigm shift that had just happened in his eyes. I was really proud of him at that moment, because such insight requires vulnerability and humility. It was beautiful to witness.

The key point for each participant can be something completely different and it will often be something they had not expected to learn. It is not uncommon to read through evaluation forms after a learning event and discover that the modules that were the most relevant for some, were the least relevant for others. We, as learning facilitators can't control, really, when it clicks. We can open doors, we can put a spotlight on different dark corners within the room beyond. But we can't make our participants step through the door.

We need to create spaces for self-reflection and critical self-examination. We can provide resources for debriefing and for peer-support. But we can't make them learn.

Specific methods or inputs will, of course, point to very specific insights. *The Spaghetti Tower Challenge*[19] points very clearly towards insights on team-design processes, collaboration and iteration. An expert's talk on a specific theory or experience will be about exactly that.

It's such a luxury to work with a group of people that has a shared sense of gap and has identified the same shortcomings and obstacles to their success. To lead them towards the key insight that will enable them to create the future they want is amazing.

Often, however, we don't have that situation.

Classrooms, lecturing halls, even training rooms rarely hold a group that are all on the same journey. Our task then as a learning facilitator is to design a path that holds space for different aha-moments. Just as Luke, Leia, Han and Chewie all had their separate journeys, literally and metaphorically, to go through, each one managed to make that round trip and emerge changed.

School and University courses, as well as open Training Courses, need to be thought of very similarly as an ensemble story, not a one hero journey like *Batman*, *Wonder Woman* or *Die Hard*, more like *The Lord of the Rings* or *The Avengers*.

Reflection Groups are a staple of international youth seminars and educational activities in the non-formal education sector. They are fairly rare, though, in international business training settings or in conferences, which is really a shame. The format is such that a set group of participants meet either on their own or with a facilitator in regular intervals and discuss different aspects of their personal learning journey. They would discuss with prompts like "What really stayed with me today is...", "If

---

[19] If you don't know it, please go ahead and Google it. There's even a TED Talk on it. It's really great.

today was a weather report, it would go like this…" or "I found myself startled or surprised today by…"

This setting, of being with other learners and discussing everyone's moments of insight, doubt, boredom or excitement can be such a catalyst for realising one's own thoughts, but also for being inspired by what others have gained.

A Learning Journal, as already mentioned, can also be an incredibly powerful tool to foster this moment of making things click. Just simply the act of sitting down and writing a few words, spending some time with the question of "What did I learn today and what does it mean to me?" can make one stop for a moment and really let things sink in.

In a multi-day event, it can be a useful strategy to start each day in small groups, discussing what each member has learned the day before and what they're bringing with them into the new day.

Questions to consider regarding the Find stage:

- What moments of self-reflection and realisation can I create in the process to foster the identification of *turning points* for participants?

- What methods can I use to visualise, verbalise or otherwise make tangible the insights that participants have generated for themselves?

TAKE - "The Incorporation"

How this works in the stories we know

In stories, *the road of trials* strips the protagonist of their limiting thoughts, self-perceptions and illusions until they see themselves and the world as it is. On the road back, they need to figure out how to bring the new, the changed paradigm, back into the light.

This is when Rey carries Finn into the Millennium Falcon after he's been badly wounded by Kylo Ren. She owns her new role and literally carries others. It's when Sam says, "I can't carry it for you, but I can carry you!" and takes him on his shoulders to deliver the ring to the lava lake. It's when Hermione in *Harry Potter and The Sorcerer's Stone*, and I'm paraphrasing here, says, "Screw it, let's go break some rules, but let's do it smartly." It's when Neo says that he has to go save Morpheus and fight Agent Smith.

At this point in the story circle, protagonists use the hard lessons they have learned on their way down and apply them. They have emerged from the darkest points and now are ready for what's to happen next.

How we can use that in the learning events we create

The *Take* phase is very similar to the *Search* phase in that it requires effort.

In learning journeys, participants need to have a chance to operationalise their learning in a way that makes sense outside the training room, back in the real world, where they have tasks and requests bombarding them from every side.

In a communication seminar, this is where managers might give each other feedback to practice the models they have learned and simulate how such a conversation might look like back at work. In a math-class, this is where students may calculate the trajectory of a rocket they are about the launch.

The action is directed towards the applicable.

During the *Take* phase, the learners need to integrate the insights they have gained into their new understanding of who they are and what they are able to do. At this point, creativity, adaptation and continuous experimentation are the modi operandi. Still in the safety of the learning environment - protected from real-world's negative consequences of mistakes. It is here that learners should receive the freedom and space they need to try out how it feels to be the person who understands what they have just learned.

This is a phase that is often overlooked in many traditional learning environments and even in business trainings, team retreats or organisational development exercises.

There is just enough time to *teach* without spending any time at all on actually doing something with those new skills, practicing together, and creatively adapting the lessons learned to the actual environment of the learners.

In order for learners to really be energised to make their insights a part of themselves, it's really important that there are strong connections between the *Take* phase, the *Search* phase, the *Need* phase and the *Change* phase. A square inside the circle, if you will. There needs to be a strong link between those four points.

The *Search* phase is all about responding to a *Need* and filling the gap between this world as it is and the world as it should be. Once we have changed, the *Take* phase is all about preparing the insights and new skills in order to make them work and fit as effectively as possible with the known world, the *Change* step of the circle.

As we have established in the very beginning - learning doesn't happen in a vacuum and the learner's worlds are crucially important to enable lasting positive change.

In the *Take* phase, we need to re-examine the learner's world with them and understand what obstacles might appear to integrate the learning into that context they're coming from.

But it's not only about searching for difficulties and addressing them, the *Take* phase also needs to look at opportunities to shine and excel using those new skills and insights.

By doing this, we already patted down the grass in the area that might become a new path and eventually a road. Transfer and transformation doesn't happen by itself, just because someone has learned something new. It happens because that someone consciously prepared for it to happen.

So what might be some examples worth considering?

The Start Stop Continue Retrospective can be very powerful here. Participants reflect individually or collectively (if they are also a team that works together outside the learning event) about some of the things they would like to start and how; some of the things they would want to stop doing and their current behaviours they want to actively continue to pursue. This works really well to empower learners to take ownership of what and how they want to make their own.

This can be super-diverse and different learners will choose to do (and stop doing) very different things. The task of the facilitator here is to keep a very close eye on where participants might either under- or over-challenge themselves and to push them to really reflect on how they are going to make the best out of what they have learned at the learning event.

Another great thing to do when you're in this step of your journey is to simply play that piece of music that you've been working on to others. Have that feedback conversation with your peers inside the course and discuss what you might need to pay attention to in the *real world*. Create a draft meeting set-up using all the skills you have acquired during the *Search* step.

In this stage, the participants really need to be in charge and essentially only be given the space by the facilitators, but no more instruction. An empty canvas on which they can play with the competences they have developed.

This is the time for creativity, for making plans and for strategizing. This can still be the time for experimentation, but with a lot more control by the participants and less structure given by the facilitator.

I've also often used the *Open Space*[20] methodology in this phase, which allows participants to say what they still need to speak about, where they still need input, or offer something that they themselves have developed in the time of the learning journey.

---

[20] Again, if you already know this methodology I do not wish to bore you with an introduction at this point. And if you don't know it, there is not enough space to really do it justice on these pages. If you are curious, I suggest searching around on the old internet, which will be full of the history, the structure and the step-by-steps of this approach.

Questions to consider regarding the Take stage:

- How can I support my participants to operationalise their insights?

- How can my participants start using their new competences still in the setting of the course?

- What methods can I think of that can simulate the participant's reality in the setting of the learning event and *rehearse* the return?

- Who or what doesn't want the participants to be their new selves in the old context?

- How can you strategize together to overcome their objections?

Phase III: Transformative Integration

RETURN - "The Integration"

How this works in the stories we know

The Blues Brothers with their full tank of gas, half a pack of cigarettes and sunglasses on drive through the night back to Chicago to pay the tax bill of the orphanage they grew up in. Frodo, Sam, Merry and Pippin ride back to the Shire and Sam is now the kind of hobbit that can have a conversation with Rosi, which he was too shy to do before the adventure. Moana comes home to her island and brings the joy of sailing and exploring back to her people. It's the conclusion of the all the complications that came before.

It's important to note that *home* doesn't need to mean back to the same place one came from. Luke doesn't go back to Tatooine and Rey doesn't go back to Jakku. They both never really fit in on those worlds. They go back *home* to the rebel base.

Returning to the known world doesn't necessarily mean going back to a context where the protagonist was unhappy before. It means going to a comfort zone, maybe even someplace that was uncomfortable before but has become comfortable as a result of the journey. This can be the new leadership role (Luke, Rey), the place on the throne (Aragorn) or the celebration in the Gryffindor common room.

How we can use that in the learning events we create

Learning is about transformation and not just the transformation of the mind of one person but the transformation of the world that person inhabits. The return to the *real* world is hard. Any young person that has ever spent a week or more in a summer camp will know the tears on the last night, when they

have to go home but know that no-one there will ever be able to understand the experiences they have made and the transformation they have gone through as they were away.

Someone who has learned how to connect and communicate with people very different to them will find it hard to transfer the techniques they have learned within the safety and insularity of the training course to the hectic and chaos of their workplace.

Not everyone has been going through the same experience as they have. Not everyone will even think that the learning they have gone through is necessary or relevant to their daily business.

What should happen after the learning event needs to be talked about, discussed and planned during the learning event. Simply walking out of the training room with a full head but an empty to do list is likely leading to an underutilisation of the learning.

We have to keep in mind that the learning process itself is not what it's about. The training room, the conference hall or the class room are not what it's all about - these are only a temporary space where new insights can be gained and then brought back to the known world where our learners actually spend most of their time in.

If we, as learning facilitators don't spend a significant amount of our creativity and planning towards making sure the learned insights actually get transferred to the daily life of our learners, we could question if we have done our job at all.

The *Return* step is right on the other side of *Go*. And they have a lot in common. Humans are reluctant to go into the unknown and expose themselves to something new, something they have not known, seen or experienced before. But once the learner has gone into the dark side of the circle and has explored, discovered and experimented, the world that was known to them is now just as scary to return to as the darkness was to enter.

Will their peers accept them with their new insights and skills? Will they be able to use their developed abilities? Or will their colleagues be happy that they had a great couple of days, but please, don't change anything around here? The learners will need just as much support and encouragement to confidently return as changed people into their known world as they have needed when we invited them to explore the new and unknown.

Similar to the *Go* phase, the *Return* phase is short and mostly unsupervised. Learners simply return to their contexts. The preparation for this happens in the Take phase and if we did a good job there, the *Return* is smooth and purposeful.

It's the morning of the next day, when we look around the office or our living room, and we are starting a new day with a (slightly) new brain. If the transition was well planned and executed, it should feel as a natural step away from the safety of the training room or class back into the job, the family or the next semester. When learners feel equipped to have an impact in the space they are going towards, then this step can be as short as a handshake and a truly meant *thank you.*

In cases where we might work with a Learning Journal during the event, it can be a great idea to give the participant a new notebook as they venture into this phase on their own. It can also be a prepared second Learning Journal that can encourage learners to keep up the habit of noting their experiences, reflecting on how they are managing the transfer and what they need to remind themselves of.

Another approach that works particularly well in courses that are a bit longer and where the group of participants has become a strong feature of the learning experience is to not give the participants their certificates of participation one-directionally from the trainer(s), but to ask the participants to give them to each other, saying a few words of appreciation and what they have gained from and wish for this person.

Questions to consider regarding the Return stage:

- How can I check if my participants are ready to transfer their competences to the world outside the learning space?

- What symbolic act can we perform to mark this transition?

- What can I do to create a feeling of beginning around this moment, rather than ending?

CHANGE - "The new normal"

How this works in the stories we know

This is the epilogue . This is the moment after the dust has settled. The Blues Brothers now make music in prison. John McClain is extremely dirty, bloody and beaten up, but he's alive and all the bad people aren't (every *Die Hard* movie). Hugh Grant and Julia Roberts are on the bench in the park, he reading, she pregnant enjoying a nap with his lab as a pillow. Rey and her friends have escaped and are setting course to their next unknown adventure (*The Last Jedi*). Aragorn is king, Sam has a family, Frodo joins Bilbo and a bunch of elves on the last ship going west. Iron Man, Captain America, Thor, the Black Widow, the Hulk and Hawkeye eat shawarma (the first *Avengers* movie, after the credits).

This is the world in which Voldemort no longer scares the heck out of the magical community. This is the world in which Sauron and Saruman are both history.

This is the world in which the management team has established a vision that propels the entire organisation. This is the world in which math is actually fun and explains the wonders of the universe.

What a wonderful world this is, right?

How we can use that in the learning events we create

Change is hard but if we've done our job right as learning facilitators, change is inevitable after having gone through the learning journey we've designed.

Every story is as much about transformation as it is learning. The change in the world that the learner now inhabits and influences was the goal all along.

The *Change* stage directly relates to the stage in parallel to the right: *Need* and just opposite *Search*. The world we have in *Change* is now hopefully what we have looked at from the other side of the gap as we have described a future that is worth going into the darkness for. And it is precisely what we have found in *Search* that will make us the master of the now in this new, old world that we have returned to.

How can we make sure that this change occurs?

In some cases and some formats, we don't. The students are not in our class anymore, the participants of our online course have finished all the segments, the participants of the conference have gone home. However, in some cases, we do have a chance to still accompany this transition and integration.

Follow-Up coaching is a great way to make sure learners can have some fairly regular check-ins to keep on track, clarify doubts or accelerate their development while embedded in their *normal* environment.

It also might make sense to form groups while still together in the learner's journey and keep those groups going in a semi-moderated way, which can meet in different intervals and report to each other on how they have been doing and what they managed to accomplish with their newly developed competences. You could call them *support groups*, but that name has a very *medical* ring to it. I prefer *check-in teams* or *home-groups*.

Questions to consider regarding the Change stage:

- What support will feel natural and make sense in my participant's world that can help them stay in touch with their insights and continue their growth?

- What kind of access will I have to my participants after our journey together? What can I realistically promise? What can they realistically accommodate?

- How can your participants really celebrate what they have learned and how can you celebrate with them?

4

Some concrete examples

A Conference   p. 125

A Management Retreat   p. 129

A Strategic Workshop   p. 135

PART IV: Some concrete examples

In the previous chapters I've given a diverse range of examples on how each step of the Learner's Journey can be achieved methodologically. To finish, I'd like to offer a few examples of my own work that can showcase how a single event that has been designed using the approaches laid out before looks like. None of them are perfect, because nothing in this world ever is. They might, however, be an interesting inspiration; a starting point for you to think about your own upcoming learning events and how to make those the best learning experiences they can possibly be.

The 2nd International Youth Volunteering Conference of UNESCO

In 2017 I was asked to help a team at UNESCO to design, plan and facilitate a three day conference for 100 people, coming from all corners of the world. The organisers wanted to do something new and interesting, but it needed to also work with the very institutional setting and environment. The participants were all young adults, who all had extensive experience as volunteering leaders of diverse youth groups, communities, social justice or art projects.

The aim of the conference was to highlight and celebrate the role Volunteerism can have in supporting human progress, but also to empower the participants through networking, competence development and the institutional connection with UNESCO to further expand the impact of their work in their contexts.

Based on the first programme proposal, we went through a large number of iterations, continuously negotiating and balancing the needs of the diverse stakeholders. As most of the stakeholders had a seat and a voice at the table, I took it as my task to take the perspective of the participants and their needs as we were discussing and shaping each programme element.

Here is what we ended up doing, using The Learner's Journey as the guiding principle.

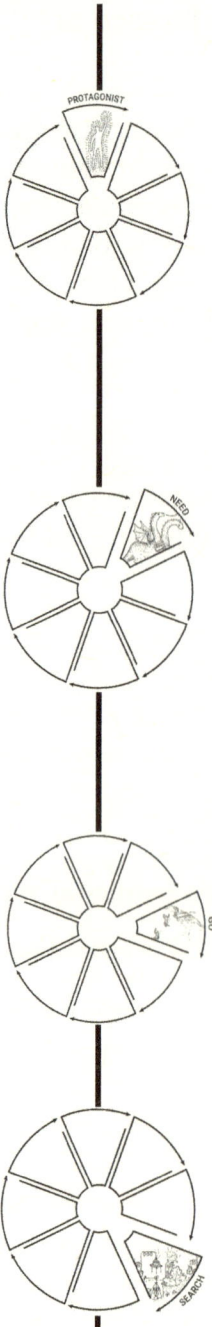

During an informal evening before the conference, we brought all the participants together for different team-building activities. We also prepared conference bags that allowed participants to write how they'd like to be addressed, what they love to talk about, what their view on volunteering was, etc. The logo of the conference was printed as an empty fractal on the bag and participants could colour it in as they wished. This shared experience sparked conversations for the rest of the night and built connections between participants on a personal level from the start.

The conference was opened by a row of high stakeholders of UNESCO. This was organised with close involvement of the protocol office of UNESCO, making sure we avoid any diplomatic offences. During the introduction of the programme, the facilitators asked participants to describe what a successful conference would be for them, what they personally would want to get out of it and what they are willing to contribute. We had participants share this with one another and collected the feedback from groups on flip charts in the front of the room.

After hearing the introductions to different thematic workshops, participants signed up for the ones that corresponded most closely to their needs and interests. Participants also placed themselves in one of four sharing places that were divided along different thematic focuses that were woven through the conference: protection of cultural heritage, intercultural education, refugees and migrants, and (social) media for dialogue.

After the lunch break, we changed the rooms to the sharing spaces, we changed the direction of input from stage-audience to peer-to-peer. During the afternoon, participants first exchanged and shared with peers who worked in the same areas they were working in. We did this to frame participants from the onset not as consumers and recipients of external experts, but as makers, creators, experts and resources for their peers. Later, they visited the spaces of other groups to learn from other areas, cross-pollinate ideas and find new inspirations.

On the next day, participants took part in training sessions that were targeted at specific skill sets and methodologies, such as theatre, sports or the Human Library.

In Working Groups, participants were then encouraged to combine their own experience with what they had learned from their peers, as well as in the training sessions. Their task was to find new ways, combine new thoughts and create something innovative that has a chance to impact lives through volunteering globally. The working groups also had input and guidance from resource persons working at UNESCO in the areas of media, cultural heritage, education and migration.

Participants then presented their ideas, perspectives and proposals to the rest of the Conference, including high-level stakeholder, as Commitments for the Future. The members of other working groups applauded each of the ideas and celebrated the innovations.

We closed the conference by presenting each participant with certificates that were personally given by the Director General of UNESCO. Empowered by this symbolic gesture and the connections they had made with fellow participants, everyone returned to their home countries.

The conference led to a row of different small scale, locally-implemented-but-internationally-connected projects. The peer-support network that was established during the conference remained tangible for many months after the event and continues to inspire the participants.

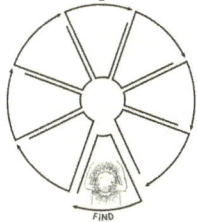

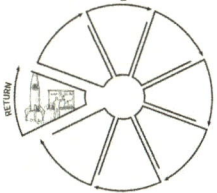

127

Authentic Authority Management Retreat for a global financial institution

On a warm Friday in September 2017, I went with the leadership team of a medium-sized division of a global financial institution on a retreat. Their challenge was that their status had been elevated within the global organisational functional structure (which is great), but many members on the team were rather inexperienced in interacting with senior leaders within the organisation. The members of the team would also have to influence those senior leaders across the entire company, but without having any formal authority over them. They would have to become masters of influencing the dotted lines upwards.

We decided to take the team out of the company context, in fact, out of town and out of any situation they would have been used to. We went to a horse sanctuary, where around 20 horses lived as a semi-autonomous herd under the watchful eye of a master in natural horsemanship. Our meetings and discussions would take place in a small house that was in the middle of the meadow, equipped with a wood-burning oven and plenty of snacks, tea and coffee. I used The Learner's Journey to think through the programme and the logical steps that would help us get to where we wanted to go.

Before the event I had phone conversations with every member of the team, gathering their perspectives and learning about their experiences in the team. At the retreat site itself, we started by having coffee together and making a round on how we felt, what our first impressions were of the space and the challenge we had set up for ourselves for the day.

The group then engaged in a Challenge Mapping exercise. I had prepared a large print out of three concentric circles. The outer layer was labelled knowledge issues, the middle one ability issues and the most central one core issues. Using post-its and markers, all the team members first reflected individually on the challenges their team faced and how to categorise them. They then discussed all the proposed views, combined and clustered until they had a clear focus and set of tangible and addressable obstacles to tackle. We then turned to the first challenge that appeared, which was around leadership and guidance towards the team members of the managers in the group. After exploring the concept of Situational Leadership, the participants reflected on their individual team members to achieve an optimal balance of empowerment and guidance and set out the first plan for each of those team members.

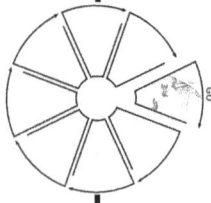

By this point it was lunchtime and the group went to a large kitchen space. Instead of eating an already prepared meal, we cooked together. In small teams, participants received recipes and started to peel, chop, fry, bake, stir and taste. While not explicitly addressed, this experience of making and sharing food together, of creating something nurturing as a team set the atmosphere for the rest of the retreat.

After the lunch break, we worked with the horses. Each participant was invited to observe the horses as they were grazing and then select the one they wanted to work with. Assisted by a horse-handler, the participants went to the horse, put on a holster and led the horses to a space on the meadow that had small obstacles prepared. This was the first challenge, as the horses would not all follow the participants without having an opinion on their own about it. The participants had to do a few exercises with the horses and afterwards sat with the horse-master to debrief and learn about how the horses react to authority, what makes them feel safe, and what enables them to trust you.

After this we went back to our little house, where we looked at the concept of Radical Candor and then practiced feedback. Each person publicly asked for and received feedback from each of their peers. This was a tough, humbling but empowering experience for everyone.

Participants then went to have some time for themselves, to sit on the grass or on a bench and look again at the feedback they have received, what it means for them and what they are planning to do about it. They had some time to just look at the horses and reflect on their time with them and what they learned about authority, trusted leadership and guidance from them.

Back in the group, participants shared their insights and made their personal developmental plans, the challenges they would take on and the support they would need from their peers. By making their plans transparent, they made themselves accountable to address them, but they also enrolled their peers as allies in their development.

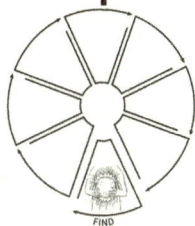

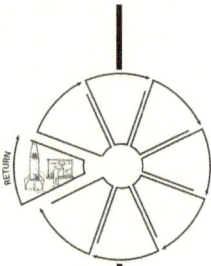

Several members of the team actually spent the night in the small house on the meadow and returned home only in the morning. They further formed bonds as they sat around a camp-fire and became closer as humans.

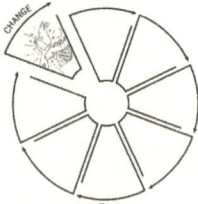

Returning to their work, the team continued to thrive and managed to influence the rest of the organisation towards positive development. Even after a while, the team continued to refer back to the insights and experiences they had shared at the retreat and it continues to be an anchor point in their collaboration.

Mission, Vision and Values Workshop for an international aviation company

For a Joint Venture in the aviation industry, I was part of a team in October of 2018 that supported the newly formed company in developing a mission, vision and values statement. The company had been created 1.5 years before and was preparing to open a big production site and expand the employee base significantly from a small start-up team to the large, fully functioning company.

Before opening the site and making their recruitment push, the leadership of the company had decided that they needed a solid and shared base upon which this growth could stand. As the Joint Venture had two different parent companies that, while both in the same industry, had significantly different histories and organisational cultures, it was deemed important to very consciously put attention on the company culture for the way forward.

In order to do this, a workshop was organised that had many of the senior leaders, but also many participants from different parts of the organisation, from front line mechanics, to engineers, team leaders and department heads.

The purpose of the workshop was to develop a mission statement together for the company that could describe what the company strived to be, a vision for the company's operations in one year, three years and five years, as well as a set of values that everyone would be happy to be held accountable to in order to live up to the mission and reach the vision.

Here's how we used The Learner's Journey to create the programme for that workshop.

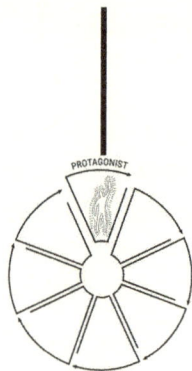

The workshop began on an afternoon, in an old barn that had been modified into a conference space. The workshop started with a welcome from the CEO and the COO, who highlighted the importance of the event and how committed they were to the results of our work. The CEO and COO would remain and very actively contribute to the workshop throughout its duration.

We then began with an exercise that asked each person to draw on a flip-chart what they look for in a team, what they can contribute, what is the most important in their life, what dreams they have, what they look for in their work and other things. We took a good long time to have each poster presented by its creator. We then saw that there were many different passions, but a strong theme of family orientation.

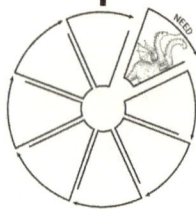

Later, we divided the group into smaller teams and did the flying-egg-challenge: each team first had to specify their expectations towards a device that would transport a raw egg over the distance of a few meters, this was passed to another team, who would design the device, which was then passed to another group to build it. In the end, the first group received their devices to test. This experience showed the importance of collaboration, communication and clarity.

On the next day, we started with a methodology called Appreciative Inquiry, which solicited from participants their best examples and experiences of working in an environment they could be proud of. Our aim would now be to achieve the same pride in our work here.

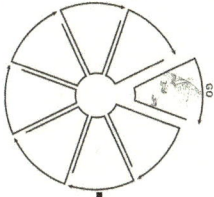

Over a coffee break, we then went from aiming and dreaming to creating. This shift was not highlighted as the progression was very natural and logical.

We divided the group in three subgroups, each with a different perspective: shareholders, customers and employees/local community. Each group drew up their ideas for who the company would be for those stakeholders. What would make it attractive, what would make them happy to be associated with this company. They discussed what vision each of those stakeholders might have for this company and what behaviours they would like to see each day in the operations and human interactions that would give them confidence. Through a row of creative work, iterations, feedback from other teams, cross-pollination sessions and other methods, we slowly worked our way to draft statements.

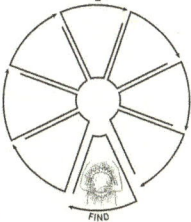

By combining the wording of different mission statements, the spirit of others, a small group of people kept working through a coffee-break to produce a final proposal for the mission statement. This was widely and enthusiastically accepted by the whole group as it reflected the discussions and input from everyone. The group also had developed a large range of concrete behaviours that they would like to see from themselves and their colleagues in all levels of the organisation and in all contexts. These ranged from safety to recognition, from feedback behaviour to safeguarding everyone's work-life balance.

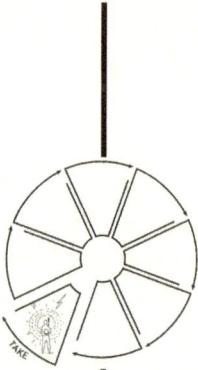

A few days after the workshop, one of us sat with the CEO and COO to structure and harmonise the input on the vision. As setting a company's vision is very much a leadership task, we felt that it was necessary that the leadership could do the final formulation on this to ensure that it hit the right balance of ambition and feasibility.

Another team continued to work on the value statements. They took the behaviour descriptions that participants at the workshop had come up with and categorised them under different headlines such as learning, well-being, and recognition. The team further polished some of the sentences, clarified them and combined others that were doubled.

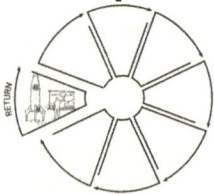

At a leadership meeting with all team and department heads, the mission, vision and value statements were then presented and discussed to make sure all the leaders were on board and ready to communicate, defend and promote these to their teams. At an all-hands meeting, they were finally presented by the CEO, COO and workshop participants.

The company committed to let their recruitment, leadership development, performance appraisal, as well as other internal processes be guided by the mission, vision and value statements that this team had collaboratively developed. It now saturates every aspect of the company.

Over to you

So, here we are. You've given me your time and I hope that I managed to fill it with words worth reading.

It's now up to you to decide if all of this was useful and practical or simply an interesting perspective to take on your work as facilitators of learning experiences and events.

It's always been up to you.

In a way, you've just completed the reader's journey and you have changed in the process, even if it's just a little bit.

I don't want to pretend that I've given you an essential guide, a solution to all the challenges that await those who dare to accompany learners on their journeys. I don't think that such a thing exists or even that it should. I would encourage you, though, to try out these suggestions and to follow the format at least once and see how it works for you.

I can't wait to meet you someday and hear how it's been.

About the Author

Bastian Küntzel lives in Wroclaw, Poland, and shares that life with an incredible woman and two extraordinary daughters. He is a bedtime-story reader, a cook and baker, a friend and a moderate introvert. As the co-founder and CEO of INCONTRO (www.incontro-training.org), he facilitates learning at the intersection of culture, communication and management.

Bastian has been involved in the training field since 1999, holds a Master's Degree in Intercultural Communication and Adult Education and now works globally with clients such as the United Nations, UNESCO, Credit Suisse, Google, EY, ABB, HP, IBM, Daimler and IKEA.

Bastian also teaches occasionally at different universities and is a board-member of SIETAR-Polska (Society for Intercultural Education, Training and Research).

You can go to **www.learners-journey.com** for resources and templates that you can use in the preparation of your learning events.

www.ingramcontent.com/pod-product-compliance
Ingram Content Group UK Ltd.
Pitfield, Milton Keynes, MK11 3LW, UK
UKHW041017250225
4747UKWH00013B/41

9 783749 419760